1993

THE AMISH COOK
COOKBOOK

By Elizabeth Coblentz

Edited by Kevin Williams
OASIS NEWSFEATURES

Illustrations by Alan Wickey

Dedication:

My sincere thanks to my daughters Leah, Verena, Liz, Lovina, Emma, and Susan for helping to make this book a success. Thanks also goes to my husband, Ben A. Coblentz, for his confident support, with gratitude and love. Thanks also to Alan S. Wickey for his illustrations in this book.

Most of all, to Kevin Williams who took his time to have this book published. Without Kevin, this book wouldn't be available.

Thanks also goes to Jim Williams for his support and time in refining this book.

From the editor's desk:

I pulled nervously into the Coblentz's driveway on a warm and windy July afternoon in the summer of 1991. A year had passed since I graduated from high school, and I had just completed my freshman year at John Carroll University in Cleveland. I had been active in the media for several years leading up to that first fateful Coblentz encounter.

After seeing a carefully-crafted handwritten cookbook in the kitchen of an Amish woman in Michigan, an idea slowly began to take shape in my mind. The handwritten cookbook struck me as very charming; something that should be shared with everyone. I went back to my Ohio home, and for months the thought of the tiny handwritten cookbook marinated in my mind. I thought of *The Budget*, the Amish-Mennonite community newspaper (see page 182), and how peaceful that paper is.

One July morning in 1991, I traveled to Michigan to ask the woman who wrote the cookbook, if she wanted to write a weekly newspaper column. It was a tough sell, asking an Amish person, by nature extremely private, to reveal herself in the mainstream media every week. The Michigan woman politely declined. I drove from house to house in southern Michigan, making my pitch to reclusive Amish women: Asking them to write a weekly newspaper column. At each house I was politely turned down. Finally, an Amish man in Reading, Michigan found a cookbook in his basement and looked up the name of the author. She was an Amish woman who lived in Indiana. So in a last attempt to find a writer, I drove south to Indiana.

When I arrived in this heavily Amish area of Indiana, I tried to locate the cookbook author that the Michigan man had told me about. I found someone who knew her, only to find out that she had left the Amish church and moved to Virginia. Dejected but determined, I continued my search.

I found a tiny roadside bakery run by an Amish woman. I thought for sure that she would be the perfect candidate to write a weekly cooking column. The baker, however, said that she was simply too busy to write.

I was frustrated and beginning to think that I would never find an Amish person willing to write a weekly column. I left the bakery, telling myself that I would turn into the first Amish driveway and just ask blindly. It was then that I stumbled upon the Coblentzes.

Elizabeth began writing her column in August of 1991, and the following month it debuted in *The Quincy* (Ill.) *Herald-Whig.* It now appears in dozens of newspapers from Kansas to Maryland to Florida.

She handwrites her column each week and sends it to Oasis Newsfeatures, where it is typed, edited, and transmitted to newspapers across the country. Elizabeth plays no role in promoting the column.

As you read this book, she is probably canning, ironing, taking care of her grandchildren or tending to the garden. Life goes on peacefully for the Coblentzes, they live their lives in tranquil anonymity despite the popularity of her column.

Some call us the odd couple of cooking, a 57-year-old Amish woman and a 21-year-old journalist. We have created this cookbook from our hearts, and tried to make it the best. Have fun with it!

TABLE OF CONTENTS

A STEP IN TIME

Tucked away in rural America is a storybook culture, where clip-clopping horse hooves and tiny sawmills, add to the tranquillity of the country. Men with long beards, dressed in wide-brimmed black hats, command horse-drawn carriages along gravelly, ribbony roads. Women, wearing plain, solid-colored dresses and white head-coverings shepherd their children safely to and from a one-room school house outside of the village.

These are the sights and sounds of the Old Order Amish.

While people may tend to idealize the Amish, and make them, undeservedly, into a saintly society, the Amish culture does have values of community, simplicity, and thrift which seem to be disappearing from the larger, mainstream world. These core values attract outsiders to the Amish.

Elizabeth Coblentz, the author of this book, is Old Order Amish. She lives with her husband and eight children in rural Indiana. They have no plumbing, electricity, or gasoline-powered motor vehicles.

Following, are Elizabeth Coblentz's own words, describing the Amish:

*The word **Amish** comes from Jacob Ammann, the name of an influential bishop of the late 1600s and early 1700s.*

Driven by persecution from their homes in Switzerland, Germany, and Alsace-Lorraine, hundreds of Amish immigrated to the new country, North America, during a period of 150 years, beginning soon after 1720.

Today, there are Amish congregations in many states. The three largest settlements of Amish are located in Holmes County, Ohio; Lancaster County, Pennsylvania; and La Grange County, Indiana.

People often ask why Amish women wear a head covering - it is obedience to the Bible, where it says: "Every woman that prayeth or prophesieth with her head uncovered dishonoreth her head," (1 Cor. 11:5).

The Amish feel that the church is responsible to care for its own poor, aged, and infirm (1 Tim. 5: 4,8) and accordingly do not accept government subsidies, welfare, or pensions.

The Amish dress as they have for centuries, and still drive their horse and buggies. Also, the Amish believe that a Christian should not take part in any violence, either in war, or in self-defense.

Elizabeth Coblentz, March 1992

A WEEK'S WORTH OF MEALS

Following is a meal diary kept for one week during the summer of 1993. It is quite typical of Amish eating habits. A blend of modern and old German meals can be found in this sampler. It was corn harvest time, as evidenced by the abundance of cob corn on the menu. Between meal snacks are a rarity for the Coblentzes, and the Amish in general.

Garden eats are plentiful which makes meal-planning so much easier at this time of year. Corn on the cob goes good on the menu for this household. The vegetables coming from the garden have a better, fresher taste.

MONDAY

Breakfast: Fried eggs, fried potatoes, toast, cheese, hot peppers, apple sauce, cookies, coffee, bananas, margarine, and jam.

Lunch: Sandwiches, hot peppers, sliced tomatoes, lettuce, cheese, and Pepsi.™

Supper: Fried chicken, mashed potatoes, gravy, macaroni and cheese, lettuce salad, dressing, sliced tomatoes, celery and carrot sticks, buttered peas, fruit salad, pie, cake, bread, margarine, and jam.

TUESDAY

Breakfast: Fried eggs, fried potatoes, toast, cheese, orange juice, coffee, rhubarb jam, margarine, and hot peppers.

Lunch: It was just Emma and I for lunch today, so we had hot dogs, cheese, hot peppers, bread and buns, sliced tomatoes, and pop.

Supper: Corn on cob, potatoes, hot dogs, cucumber salad, cheese, sliced tomatoes, bread, buns, and margarine.

WEDNESDAY

Breakfast: Fried eggs, fried potatoes, toast, cheese, orange juice, coffee, hot peppers, rhubarb jam, margarine, and snack cakes.

Lunch: Corn on cob, mashed potatoes, chili soup, crackers, sloppy joe, lettuce, pickle salad, sweet and sour pickles, hot pepper and Swiss cheese, peaches in Jello™, lemon pie, pineapples, bread and buns, rhubarb jam and margarine and snack cakes. Also, carrots and celery sticks.

Supper: Corn on cob, potatoes with peelings on, hamburger, hot peppers and Swiss cheese, lettuce, sweet and sour pickles, chili soup, crackers, Jello fruit salad, lemon pie, bread and buns, margarine, jam, celery and carrot sticks.

THURSDAY

Breakfast: Fried potatoes, fried eggs, ham, hot peppers, Swiss cheese, toast, orange juice, coffee, hot peppers, margarine, and jam.

Lunch: It was just Susan and I, so we had hot dogs, sloppy joes, chips, sliced tomatoes, Miracle Whip™, lettuce, cheese, margarine, bread and buns.

Supper: Corn on cob, potatoes with peelings on, sour cream, catsup, mustard, hot dogs, homemade pizza, sliced tomatoes, lettuce, pickles celery and carrot sticks, fruit salad, cake, pie, bread, margarine, jam, and Miracle Whip.

FRIDAY

Breakfast: Egg Dutch (omelets) with cheese on top, oatmeal, fried potatoes, sliced tomatoes, cheese, toast, jam, margarine, peaches, pineapples, bananas, and coffee.

Lunch: Homemade pizza, sliced tomatoes, sloppy joes, lettuce, potato chips, cheese, mixed fruit salad, bread, Miracle Whip, and hot peppers.

Supper: Potatoes, chunk beef, corn on cob and buttered corn, sliced tomatoes, lettuce, sour cream, hot peppers, potato chips, celery and carrot sticks, peaches with Jello, cake, and cookies.

SATURDAY

Breakfast: Coffee soup, toast, margarine, jam, bananas, cheese, and coffee.

Lunch: Homemade pizza, green beans, sliced tomatoes, cheese, buttered corn, celery and carrot sticks, lettuce, potato chips, hot peppers, peaches, and cookies.

Supper: Potatoes, chili soup, steak, corn on cob, pineapples, apple sauce, pie, potato chips, crackers, lettuce, bread, margarine, and jam.

SUNDAY

Breakfast: Egg Dutch (omelets) with cheese on top, oatmeal, fried potatoes, cheese, toast, applesauce, coffee, cookies, bacon, bananas, margarine, jam, and hot peppers.

Lunch: Mashed potatoes, beef, noodles, buttered corn, green beans, dressing, sliced tomatoes, hot peppers, celery and carrot sticks, lettuce salad, cheese, apple sauce, cookies, bread and margarine, jam, and pineapples.

Supper: Mashed potatoes, beef and noodles, buttered corn, green beans, chili soup and crackers, cheese, applesauce, lettuce, cake, pineapples, bread, jam, margarine, and sliced tomatoes.

CHANGE OF TASTE

Throughout most of the Amish existence in the United States, the Pennsylvania Dutch diet has been steady. Amish people were primarily farmers. Many Amish were almost entirely self-sufficient, with their bountiful gardens, crops, and livestock for meat.

As the occupations and sociological structures of the Amish began to change in the early 1970s and throughout the past 20 years so, too, did Amish eating habits.

The Amish began to venture into grocery stores and buy more processed and "modern foods" like chips, tuna, and soft drinks. Most of the Amish drink soda and eat chips with their meals. The Amish have borrowed these modern foods and incorporated them into their own cooking culture. Evidence of this evolution can be found throughout this cookbook. Often a recipe with call for Rice Krispies™ cereal, tuna, or a box of Hamburger Helper™.

Amish foods, which for years remained plain, are being spiced up in some communities, while retaining their simplicity. The Coblentz family was recently introduced to hot peppers, which Elizabeth laughingly calls "addictive." Simple and spicy is now popular in the Coblentz household, as Elizabeth invents new ways to use these spicy delicacies. She uses them on homemade pizza and in eggs.

Pizza has also slowly crept into the Amish diet.

Since the Amish don't have telephones to call for pizza delivery, they have to improvise by making their own. Amish pizzas, tailored to each family's tastes, are often delicious, with homemade crusts, fresh toppings, and innovative ingredients. The pizza pies are baked in wood-fired ovens.

THE LORD'S PRAYER

"Our Father who are in heaven,
Hallowed be thy name;
Thy kingdom come;
Thy will be done;
In earth, as it is in heaven.
Give us this day, our daily bread.
And forgive us our debts as we forgive our debtors.
And lead us not into temptation;
But deliver us from evil.
For thine is the kingdom, and power,
and the glory Forever.

PENNSYLVANIA DUTCH TRANSLATION:

*Unser vater der du bist im himmel,
geheiliget werde dein name zu komme
uns dein reich, dein ville geschehe auf
erden vie im himmel, gib uns heit
unser täglich brod, und vergib uns
unsere schuld, vie wir vergeben
unsern schuldern; und las uns nicht
eingeführt werden in verschung,
sondern erlöse uns von dem bösen;
denn dein ist das reich, dein ist die
kraft, dein ist die herrlichkeit in
ewigkeit. Umen.*

SOUPS

CHAPTER 1

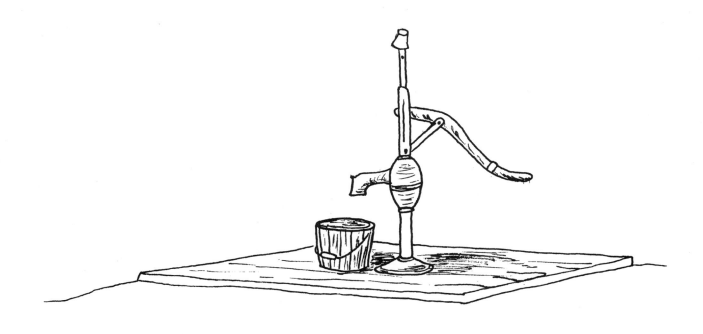

EMMA'S RAINY DAY SOUP

4 pounds of meat and bones or any bits of leftover meat
5 quarts of cold water
1 tablespoon of salt
2 stalks celery
2 onions
1 turnip
1 carrot
4 cloves
1 teaspoon parsley
1/2 teaspoon thyme
1 teaspoon savory

After rinsing the meat and bones, put it into a clean kettle and cover with cold water. Add salt and let it heat slowly until the fat rises - skim well. Let it simmer until time to strain it, cut the vegetables in slices or bits and fry them in an ounce of butter until light brown; add them to the soup with the spice and herbs. Cook all one hour; strain through a fine cheesecloth. The soups should stand until the grease settles on top, then skim every particle off. Thirty minutes before serving; set it back over the fire and heat. Serve hot.

CREAM OF CHICKEN SOUP

1/4 cup of margarine
5 tablespoons of flour
3 chicken bouillon cubes
1 cup of half and half cream

3 cups of boiling water
1/2 cup of finely chopped chicken

Melt margarine in a one quart saucepan over low heat. Blend in flour. Dissolve bouillon cubes in boiling water. Gradually add to flour and margarine mixture. Stir until smooth. Add chicken and bring to a boil over medium heat. Stir in half and half. Additional seasoning may be added. Serves six.

GARDEN VEGETABLE SOUP

2 tablespoons of butter
1 cup of potatoes, diced
2 cups of tomato juice
2 cups of milk
1/4 cup of flour
1 onion, chopped

1/2 cup of celery, chopped
1 cup of diced carrots
1 1/2 teaspoons of salt
1 pound of hamburger

Brown meat and onion in butter. Drain grease. Add remaining ingredients, but reserve the milk and flour. Cook vegetables until they are nice, soft, and done. Mix the milk and flour and stir until smooth. Add to soup and cook until thickened.

SAVORY CHILI SOUP

2 pounds of hamburger
1 cup of chopped onion
2 quarts of tomato juice
1 1/2 quarts of water
1 quart of cooked kidney beans
1/2 cup of sugar
3/4 teaspoon of chili powder
salt to taste
1/8 teaspoon of red pepper (optional)
4 rounded tablespoons of cornstarch, enough to thicken to satisfaction

Sauté onion and hamburger until brown. Drain grease. Warm tomato juice, sugar, chili powder, salt, and water to the boiling point. Save some water to dissolve cornstarch. Add hamburger and cornstarch and stir until thickened. Add beans. Cook for 5-10 minutes.

YODER'S PEA SOUP

1 cup of dried, green split peas
a ham bone (beef knuckles also can be used)
1 medium onion, chopped
1 1/2 quart of water
1 bay leaf
1 teaspoon of salt
1/2 teaspoon of pepper
1/2 cup of chunked tomatoes may be added

Put all the ingredients into a big pot. Simmer 2 hours - stirring intermittently. Add boiling water if the soup gets too thick a consistency. Remove the bone. Press the soup through a sieve and serve.

SUNDAY SOUP

1 meaty beef soup bone
1 pound of noodles
2 diced stalks of celery
1 onion, chopped
salt and pepper
4 large potatoes, chopped

Cook the beef bone with the onion and celery in 4 quarts of water until the meat is juicy and soft. Extract the meat from the broth and the bones. Set in a separate bowl. Add noodles and potatoes to the nice, boiling broth and cook until done. Put the set aside meat back into the mixture. Season with salt and pepper. Serve.

POT PIE SOUP

3 sliced potatoes
2 cups of flour
1/2 teaspoon of salt
1 egg
water
Sausage or ham broth

Put egg in a cup. Fill half-way with water. Add flour. Mix as for a pie dough. Roll thin and cut in squares. Put sausage or ham broth in a kettle and bring to a boil. Drop in squares of the rolled out dough. Add three diced up potatoes to the broth. Cook on medium for about 10 minutes.

AUNT LOVINA'S BEEF STEW

Cook a beef bone in water till done. Then add a couple of diced potatoes and some shredded cabbage. Cook and season with salt and pepper. Diced carrots can also be added. Beef broth will do if a beef bone is not available.

AMISH BEAN SOUP

1 cup of soup beans
2 tablespoons of margarine
1 quart of milk
season with salt and pepper

Cook one cup of soup beans in water (water should be one inch over beans) till done. Then stir in 2 tablespoons of margarine and 1 quart of milk. Season with salt and pepper. Pour mixture over crumbled stale bread in a bowl. Crackers can also be used instead of bread.

KITCHEN UTENSILS

Some kitchen utensils get used more often than others in our house. The spoons to stir the food, the rolling pin to roll out those pie crusts and rolls or for making pot pies; the potato masher, the turner to fry the eggs, the cheese slicer, and the vegetable grater are just a few of the tools that I use. The list can go on and on when you're preparing a meal. These are stored in the drawers of our sink, where they are washed, rinsed, and wiped by a kitchen towel.

When I was a young girl, we made noodles so often. The noodles were rolled out by the rolling pin and now we have what you call a noodle maker. It is so much easier and faster to run 100 eggs made into noodles through the noodle maker - and less tiresome. We didn't have a meat or cheese slicer as this was done by a knife.

The noodle maker is operated by a hand-crank, but still speeds up the process which used to be done entirely by hand.

The pressure cooker does its great part to process the canned goods, especially for meats, corn, green beans, soups, or whatever.

KITCHENS - Continued

Amish kitchens vary from region to region. Some kitchens are more cluttered than others. Some have barely a spoon in sight. In southern Michigan, bowls hang from racks on the ceilings and all the kitchen accessories are in view (ladles hanging from cabinets) - yet done in an orderly fashion.

In Adams County, Ohio, the Old Order Amish are permitted by local bishops to have plumbing. So water has to be brought in by the bucket from outside wells. Plumbing is the exception among the Amish, but it is slowly gaining acceptance within the church.

An abundance of Mason jars are always on hand for quick canning. The Amish have the same silverware sets that most Americans use: China for special occasions, a set of family-style dishes for casual eating, and a supply of paper plates for lazy days. Tupperware™ is a common sight in Amish kitchens. The smell of freshly baked bread often lingers in the air. Bread recipes vary from region to region. Rhubarb bread and rhubarb is a staple in the diets of most Amish - and the smell of rhubarb is a sure signal of spring.

POTATO SOUP

3 or 4 large potatoes, cut-up
1 medium onion
2 tablespoons of margarine
1 quart of milk
Variation: Some people add noodles to this soup.

Cut-up potatoes and one medium onion in water and cook together till done. Then mash them with a potato masher. Add seasoning of salt and pepper to your taste and add 2 tablespoons of margarine and 1 quart of milk. Cook until potatoes are tender. Serve with crackers.

INDIANA CHILI SOUP

.1 1/2 pounds of ground beef
3 cups of tomato juice
1 can of kidney beans
2 medium onions
1 tablespoon of chili powder
1/4 - 1/2 cup of brown sugar
salt to taste

Brown hamburger and onion in a deep pot. Add remaining ingredients and bring to a boil. Spaghetti can also be cooked and added to the soup. Cook until spaghetti is done, about 5-10 minutes on medium high.

GERMAN RIVVEL SOUP

1 quart of beef broth
1 egg, well-beaten

1 cup of flour
1/4 teaspoon of salt

Bring broth to a boil. In another bowl, combine flour, salt, and egg until mixture is crumbly. Rub through hands into boiling broth. Cook about 10 minutes on a medium heat. Rivvels look like boiled rice when cooked. You may use milk instead of broth if you wish.

MUSHROOM SOUP

1/2 pound of mushrooms
1 small onion
2 cups of chicken broth
3 tablespoons of butter
3 tablespoons of flour
1 1/2 cups of milk
1/2 cup of cream
salt and pepper

In a saucepan, put chopped mushrooms with onion - add broth and simmer covered for 15 minutes. Melt butter and stir in flour. Add milk and cook, stirring until thickened. Add cream into the mushrooms. Heat gently and season with salt and pepper until mushrooms are tender.

CHEESY BROCCOLI SOUP

1/4 cup of chopped onion
1 tablespoon of margarine
1 1/2 cups of milk
3/4 pound of processed cheese, cubed
10 ounces of frozen chopped broccoli
dash of pepper

In a 2-quart saucepan, cook onions in margarine until tender. Add remaining ingredients and stir over low heat until processed cheese is melted and mixture is hot.

Note: Any kind of cheese can be used in this soup. Cheddar is good.

SOUP TIPS:
· Always cook broth well before adding the other ingredients.
· If I boil potatoes, I use the leftover water for soup; it tastes better.
· If the soup gets too thick add more water.

COFFEE SOUP

My 88-year-old mother still enjoys this meal in the mornings.

Crumble one slice of bread into a cup. Fill with steaming coffee. Add sugar and cream and stir.

AUNT SARAH'S BROCCOLI AND CAULIFLOWER SOUP

2 cups of broccoli
2 cups cauliflower
1/2 cup of water
1 teaspoon of salt
1/2 teaspoon of basil
2 tablespoons of butter

2 1/2 tablespoons of flour
3 cups of milk

Blend broccoli, cauliflower, salt, and basil over medium heat. Cook until tender. In separate pan, melt butter until lightly browned. Add flour and stir until smooth. Gradually add milk, stirring constantly until thickened. Pour over vegetable mixture and stir until blended.

QUICK BREAD SOUP

Rip several slices of bread into chunks, or cut into cubes. Place in a bowl. Sprinkle sugar over the bread - how little or much you desire. Pour milk over bread. Berries can be added for flavor. Stir and serve.

SWISS BROCCOLI SOUP

1/4 cup of all-purpose flour
10 ounces of garden fresh or frozen broccoli
1 cup of shredded Swiss cheese
1/8 teaspoon of ground nutmeg
2 teaspoons of instant chicken bouillon granules

2 cups of milk
2 cups of water

In a large saucepan, heat chicken granules in 1 1/2 cups of water until it is dissolved. Add broccoli, cover and cook 8-10 minutes, or until tender. Add milk, cheese, nutmeg, and a dash of pepper. Cook until cheese melts. Combine flour with 1/2 cup of cold water and add to soup. Cook and stir until thickened and bubbly. Serves 4-6.

CHEESE SOUP

1/2 cup of finely chopped onion
1/2 cup of flour
4 cups of chicken broth
1/2 cup of finely diced celery
1 cup of diced, sharp cheese

4 teaspoons of butter
4 cups of milk
1/2 cups of finely diced carrots
dash each of salt and pepper

Cook onion in butter until tender. Blend in flour. Add remaining ingredients except cheese. Cook on high and stir till thickened and bubbly. Reduce heat. Add cheese, stir to melt. Simmer 15 minutes. Serves 8.

VELVETY CHEESE SOUP

1/4 cup of butter
1/4 cup of minced onion
1/4 cup of flour

1 cup of grated cheddar cheese
10 ounce package of mixed vegetables
4 cups of milk

Melt butter in saucepan. Add onions and sauté until onions are clear. Remove from heat. Blend in flour, milk, and salt to taste. Cook until thick, stirring constantly. Add cheese and stir until melted. Add cooked vegetables. Let simmer for awhile. Your own vegetables from the garden can be added: corn, peas, carrots, or whatever you wish.

CHICKEN RICE SOUP

1 whole chicken (cooked and bones removed)
2 quarts of water
1 onion, chopped
3/4 cup of celery
1 1/2 teaspoons of salt
dash of pepper
1 cup of cooked rice

Mix in a sauce pan and warm thoroughly over medium heat.

"We aren't really any different from anyone else - we all pray to the same God,"

——— An Amish woman at the Hillside Bakery in Arthur, Illinois

SALADS

CHAPTER 2

24-HOUR CABBAGE SLAW

1 head of cabbage   2 green peppers
4 onions   4 red peppers

Shred the above, bring to a boil in a pot of water. Boil for just a few minutes, and then remove. Place into a bowl, and pour the following ingredients on top:

1 pint of vinegar   1 /4 teaspoon of turmeric
2 1/2 cups of sugar   1 1/2 teaspoons of mustard seed
1 tablespoon of salt   1 teaspoon of celery seed

Stir. Let stand 24 hours. Ready to eat.

CRYSTAL SALAD

1 package of lemon juice   1/2 cup of diced apples, with peelings
1 1/4 cup of water   1/2 cup of diced pineapples
1/2 cup of pineapple juice   1/2 cup diced celery
1/2 cup of whipped cream   6 marshmallows (cut-fine)
1/2 cup of your favorite salad dressing

Dissolve the lemon gelatin in hot water. Add pineapple juice. Let set all the way. Fold in whipped cream, salad dressing, apple, pineapple, celery, and marshmallows (colored marshmallows make the salad more attractive). Serves 8-10 people.

SUMMER SALAD

1 head of lettuce, cut-up   8 red radishes, sliced thin
1 stalk of celery, cut-up   2 tomatoes, diced
1 carrot, shredded

Mix and pour the dressing of your choice over it. Some cut-up cheddar cheese and a crumbled hard-boiled egg can be mixed into the salad.

COTTAGE CHEESE SALAD

1 pound of marshmallows   1/2 cup of milk

In a saucepan, melt the above, then add 1 large package of cream cheese. Stir until melted, cool. Add:

1 can of drained, crushed pineapples
1 cup of whipped cream

Stir very well.

Fold in: 1/2 cup of chopped pecans   1 quart of cottage cheese.
Makes 3 quarts of ready-to-serve salad.

AUTUMN SALAD

2 cups of diced apples   1 cup of grated carrots
1/2 cup of raisins   1/2 cup of mayonnaise

Peel apples and dice. Add grated carrots and raisins. Using 2 spoons to mix salad, add mayonnaise. Serves 4.

BROCCOLI SALAD

1-2 heads of fresh broccoli, chopped back to a large stem
10-12 slices of crisp bacon (crumbled)
3-4 hard-cooked eggs (diced)   onion to taste

Stir the above in a bowl.
Dressing: 1/2 cup of mayonnaise, 2 tablespoon of vinegar, and 1/2 cup of sugar. Mix the dressing ingredients and stir into the broccoli mixture. Serve.

HINT - Cut back on bacon and dressing, according to the amount of broccoli that you have.

SHINY BLACK BUGGIES

We have the open, horse-drawn buggies in our community. Some areas have the covered buggies, or what is called a "top buggy." Top buggies are enclosed and probably have no blankets inside to dry afterwards when it is raining, snowing, or whatever. We use an umbrella to protect us from getting wet. In the wintertime, the umbrella really holds off the cold wind.

We have a license plate for each buggy. The slow-moving triangle emblem is also on the back end of the buggy along with reflectors of various colors. Most buggies have two blinkers and some have the flashers. It pays to be well-lighted on these busy roads.

The buggy consists of one long seat, when the family is small. Some have two and three seats on a buggy when there's a larger family. They still usually own a one-seater for when the whole family doesn't go somewhere. Years ago, they used to have string seats on their buggies, but not many are seen with string seats anymore.

The charcoal black Amish buggies are difficult to discern in the dark of night. Following are some tips for safer driving in Amish country:

1. Dim car headlights when approaching a buggy at night. Bright headlamps scare the horses.

2. Drive slowly, and be alert for horse-drawn buggies over the crests of hills. An accident in the summer of 1991 near Mount Vernon, Ohio resulted in the deaths of six Amish people, four of them children, when a speeding truck topped a hill and plowed into the group.

WILTED LETTUCE

5 slices of bacon, diced and cooked crispy
1 beaten egg
2 tablespoons of sugar
2 tablespoons of water
1/4 cup of minced onions
1/2 teaspoon of salt
1/3 cup of vinegar
6 cups of lettuce

Combine egg, onion, sugar, salt, vinegar, and water. Add to bacon and drippings. Heat just until boiling, stirring constantly. Pour over lettuce leaf or torn pieces of lettuce and toss lightly. Serve at once.

HOLMES COUNTY COLE SLAW

1 large, shredded head of cabbage
1 cup of diced celery
1/2 cup of chopped onion
1 green pepper, cut-up

1 teaspoon of celery seed
1/2 teaspoon of mustard seed
2 cups of white sugar
1/2 cup of vinegar

Blend all of the above ingredients and let it set a few hours before serving. Then refrigerate.

HOT CHICKEN SALAD

2 cups of cooked, cubed chicken
2 cups of chopped celery
1/2 cup of slivered, toasted almonds
crushed potato chips
2 tablespoons of lemon juice
1 1/2 cups of shredded cheddar cheese
2 teaspoons of chopped onion
1 cup of salad dressing

Mix all ingredients except potato chips. Put in a 2 quart casserole dish. Sprinkle chips on top. Bake 15-20 minutes at 400°.

LAYERED LETTUCE SALAD

1 head of lettuce
1/2 cup of celery
1/2 cup of chopped green pepper
1/2 cup of chopped onion
1 box of frozen peas

1 pint of real mayonnaise
2 tablespoons of sugar
8 ounces of grated cheese
8 strips of crispy bacon

Shred lettuce in bottom of a 9 X 13-inch pan. Layer, one at a time, the celery, onion, green pepper, peas, mayonnaise, bacon, and cheese.
Chill over night.

EMMA'S OWN OVERNIGHT SALAD

1 head of lettuce
1 head of cauliflower
frozen peas (quantity to your taste)
8-12 crumbled strips of crispy bacon

1 onion
carrots, (to your taste)
cheese, (to your taste)

Cut and mix together the above ingredients. Stir together salad dressing and sugar; put on top. Then add bacon bits and cheese; not too much bacon, as it gives a strong taste.

DID YOU KNOW?

- All Amish are bilingual. They speak a blend of high German and Swiss. The Germanic dialect is known as Pennsylvania Dutch. As children they are taught Pennsylvania Dutch first, English is learned as a second language. At home, among themselves, most Amish speak Pennsylvania Dutch.

- The westernmost Amish settlement in the United States is in Rexford, Montana.

COBLENTZ KITCHEN WALDORF SALAD

2 large apples
1/2 cup chopped celery
1/3 cup chopped grapes

1/4 cup of nutmeats
1/4 cup of mayonnaise
4 large marshmallows

Dice the ingredients. Mix in a bowl. Moisten with mayonnaise.

SEVEN LAYER SALAD

1 head of lettuce, chopped
2 cups of frozen peas or cauliflower
1 medium onion, sliced
hard-boiled eggs, to your taste
celery, if desired
1 pound of bacon, fried and chopped

In the bottom of a 2 quart casserole dish, layer the lettuce along the bottom, peas next, then the onion, until you have layered all the ingredients.

Seventh Layer: Spread on top, 2 cups of mayonnaise and 1/3 cup of sugar. Do not stir. Chill for 12 hours. Before serving, sprinkle with cheese.

WATERGATE SALAD

This salad is not named after the infamous Nixon scandal. Watergate refers to the irrigation systems of early Pennsylvania and Europe.

1 box of instant pistachio pudding
1 can of crushed pineapple with juice
2 or 3 cups of mini-marshmallows
1 (7 ounce) carton of whipped cream
1 cup of nuts

Mix all together. Serve.

AMISH POTATO SALAD

6 cups of potatoes, diced
6 eggs
1/4 medium onion, chopped fine
2 teaspoons salt
1/4 cup milk

1 scant tablespoon of mustard
1/4 cup of vinegar
1 1/4 cup of white sugar
3/4 cup of cut-up celery
1 1/2 cups of salad dressing

Cook potatoes in skins, not quite soft. Chill till cold. Put through salad maker. Mash boiled eggs with potato masher. Add cut-up celery as you like. This is keeps for several days.

Note: The Amish use hand-cranked "salad makers." Simply dicing the potatoes will give the same effect.

CUCUMBER SOUR CREAM SALAD

1 tablespoon of sugar
1 1/2 teaspoon of salt
1 cup of dairy sour cream
4 1/2 cups of thinly sliced, pared cucumbers

3 tablespoons of grated onion
2 tablespoons of white vinegar

Blend together sugar, salt, sour cream, onion, and vinegar in a bowl. Add cucumbers and mix well. Cover, chill at least 2 hours.

FRIENDSHIP SALAD

1 cup of diced ham
2 cups of cooked macaroni
1 1/2 tablespoons of barbecue sauce
1/4 cup of chopped grated pepper
salt and pepper to taste

1/4 cup of chopped onions
3 tablespoons of mayonnaise
3/4 cup of grated cut celery
1 teaspoon of prepared mustard
1/2 cup of chopped carrots

Combine ham, macaroni, celery, carrots, pepper, and onion. In another bowl, mix in mayonnaise, barbecue sauce, catsup, and mustard. Mix thoroughly and add to other mixture.

EXPRESS SALAD

16 ounces of cottage cheese
1-3 ounce package of orange Jello
4 1/2 ounces of Cool Whip™
1 can of drained, crushed pineapples.

Mix all ingredients together in a bowl (including dry Jello), and it is ready to serve immediately.

TACO SALAD

1 medium head of lettuce, shredded
1/2 medium onion, diced
2-3 tomatoes, cubed
1 can of drained, red kidney beans
1 pound of browned, cooked, and drained hamburger
3/4 pound of grated Cheddar cheese

Toss the above ingredients together. Mix the following ingredients separately:

1 bottle of Thousand Island dressing   1/2 bottle of catsup
2 tablespoons of sugar
1 package of taco seasoning mix

Toss the dressing with the salad. Add 1 package of taco-flavored chips. Toss again and serve.

The largest Old Order Amish population lives in the peaceful hills of Holmes County, Ohio - about 25,000 Amish. The Amish church has over 100,000 members in the U.S. and Canada.

VERENA'S DANDELION SALAD

1 pound of dandelion greens
1/4 pound of unsliced bacon
2/3 cup of light, sweet cream or half and half
4 tablespoons of vinegar
4 tablespoons of sugar, or to taste
1 tablespoon of flour
salt and pepper to taste
2 hard-boiled eggs, peeled and coarsely chopped

Wash greens and pick over carefully, removing all stray brown stands and tough stems. Trim off wilted or darkened portions. Dry thoroughly in a clean towel and keep in a slightly warmed bowl at room temperature. Cut bacon into thin strips and fry until crisp and brown. Drain bacon and crumble into small nuggets. Reserve fat in the pan. Combine cream, vinegar, sugar, flour, salt, and pepper and beat with a whisk until smooth. Pour into hot fat and bring to a boil, stirring constantly with a whisk until smooth and thick. Adjust seasoning. Pour over dandelion greens, add bacon and toss to coat greens. Garnish with chopped eggs and serve. Makes 4-6 servings.

Note: Amish children frolic in fields that are untreated by lawn-beautifying pesticides. Be sure to select your dandelions away from areas treated chemically.

SUSAN'S FROZEN FRUIT SALAD

1 large container of Cool Whip
1 can of Eagle Brand™ sweetened condensed milk
1 large can of crushed pineapples
2 small cans of mandarin oranges
1 can of cherry pie filling
2 cups of mini-marshmallows

Mix all ingredients together in a large bowl. Pour into a 9X13 pan and freeze. Thaw slightly before serving.

FRUIT PIZZA

First Layer:

3/4 cup of brown sugar
1/2 cup of melted margarine
1 egg, beaten
1 teaspoon of vanilla
1 teaspoon of lemon flavoring
1 teaspoon of baking powder
1 1/4 cup of flour

Mix and spread with knife on a 13X17 lightly greased pizza pan. Bake at 300-325° for about 20 minutes. After baking the crust, add the second and third layers.

Second Layer:

8 ounces of Cool Whip
8 ounces of cream cheese
3/4 cup of powdered sugar

Mix together, spread on the first layer.

Third Layer:

Put the following ingredients in a bowl:
1 unpeeled red apple, sliced
1 unpeeled yellow apple, sliced
1 can of pineapple, drained, save juice
1 cup of nuts
handful of red grapes, cut in half
handful of white grapes, cut in half

Take juice of pineapple and add 3/4 cup of water, 2 tablespoons of clear gelatin and 3/5 cup of sugar. Heat and bring to a boil. When cold, pour over fruit. Mix altogether and pour over second layer.

PARADISE FRUIT BOWL

2 small boxes of vanilla pudding (not instant)
2 small boxes of tapioca pudding (not instant)
1-20 ounce can of pineapple tidbits
1-16 ounce can of mandarin oranges
1 small jar of maraschino cherries
3 large bananas, sliced
1 teaspoon of orange extract

Drain and reserve all the juices from the fruits in a big bowl. Add enough water to make 6 cups of fruit liquid. In a large saucepan, combine juices and puddings. Mix well. Cook and stir until it is at a full boil on medium heat. Remove from heat and stir in orange extract. Cool well. Add fruit and refrigerate. Add bananas just before serving. Mix well.

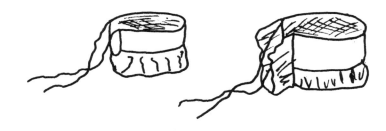

THE AMISH WEDDING

When we have weddings, we invite some women relatives and friends two days before the event to help with the baking of pies. The women also spend time making a special wedding pastry called a "nothing." Bread is toasted for the dressing and numerous other duties are completed. The scent of freshly baked pies and cooking food fills the house.

The day before the wedding, we have about six girls come to our house to peel potatoes, cut-up chicken (if chicken is on the menu), help set tables, and prepare for the company. It is lots of work, but enjoyable. Hundreds of relatives and friends show up at our weddings.

The bride and groom have two couples for their attendants and have 10 to 15 unmarried couples to wait on the tables. When we got married we had seven couples for table waiters. They usually have many more these days.

In Lancaster County, Pennsylvania and some other Amish settlements the grooms wear bow ties to the wedding - one of the few times Amish men wear ties in their lives.

The tablewaiter girls wear a light blue dress and white cape and apron. The brides in different Amish communities wear different colored dresses. In some conservative Indiana settlements the Amish brides wear a black dress, with a white cape and apron. In Lancaster County, the women are buried in the same dress.

Rings are a part of the Amish wedding, but not in the same way as their English counterparts. A ring is stuck in the wedding cake. When it is cut in the evening to pass around for young people and the family - someone usually finds the ring in their cake, and it's theirs to keep.

Note: Non-Amish people are often referred to as "English" by Amish people. In Lancaster County and some other places, non-Amish are referred to as "Yankee." This helps define the separateness between the cultures.

The wedding usually begins around 9 a.m. The bride and groom are put into marriage by noon. A large lunch and evening meal is served. The visiting with friends and eating usually continue well into the night.

If they have a place of their own, the young couple will move into their new home right after the wedding. Some go back and forth staying with one or the other set of parents till they get a home.

AMISH WEDDING RECIPE

NOTHINGS

1 egg
3 cookspoons (generous tablespoons) of cream
pinch of salt
all purpose flour as needed
vegetable shortening or lard for deep-frying
Powder sugar for sprinkling

Beat the egg to blend and stir in cream (approx. 3 generous tablespoons), salt and enough flour to make a stiff dough.

Divide into six or seven balls and roll each dough ball flat - very thin. Cut three slits, 2 inches long, in each piece.

Have a kettle of hot lard or Crisco™ ready. Put one piece at a time into the kettle. Turn over with two forks when you see a slight golden color. Take out and put on a plate covered with paper towels to drain. Then put on another plate and sprinkle with sugar. Stack all nothings on one plate. *Some Amish also call these pastries "knee patches."*

Leah's Wedding Menu

Here are the goodies prepared for the wedding dinner and supper of my oldest daughter Leah.

Chicken and noodles (cooked six big old hens)
100 quarts of mashed potatoes
Over 250 pounds of fried chicken
Corn (from our own canned corn cache)
Dressing (toasted 12 loaves of bread, plenty for both meals)
150 pounds of boneless ham
Five gallons of pork and beans
Carrot salad (used 42 boxes of orange Jello)
Potato salad - 32 quarts
24 heads of lettuce
Gravy
30 pounds of cheese
Fruit salad (from our own canned stockpiles)
Tapioca pudding (cooked 10 pounds with Jello, 12 cans of Rich's™ topping)
88 pies (cherry, raisin, and pumpkin)
33 cakes
Over 900 cookies
15 batches of nothings
Our own canned pickles
15 or 16 celery stalks
bread, coffee, jam, apple butter, margarine
Over 700 candy bars

EIGHT IS NOT ENOUGH

Feeding a family of eight was enjoyable. Five of our eight children are married now. How nice it would be to still have them all in our care, but that's life. You can expect your children to leave and start a family of their own. It is always enjoyable to see them drive in for a meal. We don't need a "welcome" sign on our door! They are always welcome, as everyone knows.

We have two boys: Amos and Albert. Our six girls are: Leah, Verena, Liz, Lovina, Emma, and Susan. Leah is married and they have two boys and two girls. Amos is married, they have five girls and one boy - this includes a set of twin girls. This is something special to our family, as neither my husband's nor my family have sets of twins. Albert is married, and they have three boys and one girl. Liz is married, and they have one girl. Daughter Lovina was just married.

When we all get together, we enjoy chicken, barbeque, mashed potatoes, homemade noodles, and all kinds of salads. We pretty well all agree on what we like and dislike when it comes to food. I enjoy baking and preparing what the family enjoys.

BREADS, ROLLS, AND DOUGHNUTS

CHAPTER 3

AMISH OVENS

The Amish do their baking in wood-fired ovens or ranges. Often Amish women will say: "bake bread in a slow oven." Baking temperatures are an inexact science among the Amish, although mobile oven thermometers in recent years have helped. The thermometers are simply mounted inside of an oven, and they can indicate whether the temperature is at 350° or whatever the desired temperature is. Following is a brief conversion chart:

100°   Warm Oven
200° - 325°   Slow Oven
325° - 400°   Medium Oven
400° - 600°   Very Hot Oven

MYSTERY BISCUITS

2 cups of sifted flour
1 tablespoon of baking powder
1 teaspoon of salt
1/4 cup of mayonnaise
1 cup of milk
1 teaspoon of sugar

Sift flour, baking powder, and salt. Add remaining ingredients. Mix till smooth and drop by tablespoons on greased cookie sheet or fill 12 muffin tins 2/3 full. Bake 18-20 minutes at 375°.

SUNDAY SERVICES

The Old Order Amish hold church services in the homes of congregation members - there is no formal church house.

Church services have been announced here, so there's a lot of cleaning to do. The walls, ceilings, and woodwork are being washed off. Some furniture has to be varnished and some painting takes place. The sinks and cupboards are being cleaned out and the dishes in them are being washed. The garden needs to be hoed and weeded, the lawn mowed, and the barns and sheds cleaned up. The list goes on and on. Everything gets a thorough cleaning. Sometimes canning is done at that time. Church services start at 9 a.m. and let out by noon. Songs are all sung in German from our song books called *Ausbund.* There are four ministers in each church district: a bishop, a deacon, and two ministers. The bishop is the leader of each church district and determines the *ordnung. Ordnung*are is an unwritten but faithfully followed set of rules that every church member follows in daily life (i.e. no television, etc.). Some rules vary from district to district because different bishops have different rules.

CHURCH SERVICES - Continued

Church districts are subdivided into sections. Each church has what you call a bench wagon. It stores the church benches and goes from place to place. The wagon protects those varnished benches better than in past years when we didn't have the covered wagons.

After church services, a noon lunch is served to all those who attended. The meals may vary from place to place. There's usually coffee, bread, jams and jellies, red beets, pickles, bologna or ham, cheese, and a peanut butter mixture which consists of corn syrup and marshmallow creme. Some also serve lettuce and tomatoes, when in season, cottage cheese, and cake.

We have four folding tables set up for church, they seat 42 at one time. Two tables are for menfolk and boys and the other two are for women and girls. The host family and single girls take care to make sure plenty of food stays on the tables and clears the dishes. There are usually between 20-30 familes in each church district (sometimes more). Each family takes their turn to have services in their home, usually about once a year.

SOURDOUGH BISCUITS

1 cup of sourdough
2 tablespoons of melted shortening
1 cup of flour
1/2 teaspoon of salt
1/2 teaspoon of baking soda
2 teaspoons of baking powder

Add shortening to sourdough. Mix. Then add remaining ingredients. Mix until you get a dough. Remove dough from bowl. Roll until 1/2 inch thick. Cut out biscuits. Let rise for 15 minutes, then bake for 15 minutes in a greased pan at 350°.

ICE CHEST ROLLS

1 cup of shortening
1 cup of sugar
1 1/2 tablespoons of salt
1 cup of boiling water
2 eggs
2 packages or 2 tablespoons of yeast
1 cup of warm water
6 cups of flour

Pour boiling water over first three ingredients. Blend and cool. Add beaten eggs. Sprinkle yeast into 1 cup of warm water and stir until dissolved. Add to mixture. Add flour. Mix well. Cover and place in refrigerated area for at least four hours - no more than a week. Shape and let rise 3 hours. Bake on greased pan at 400° for 12-15 minutes. Makes 36 rolls.

ONE HOUR ROLLS

2 cakes of yeast (or 2 packages of dry yeast)
1/4 cup of lukewarm water
1 1/4 cups of milk
3 tablespoons of sugar
1/2 teaspoon of salt
4 tablespoons of butter
3 cups of flour

Dissolve yeast in water. Milk, sugar, salt, and butter should be put into a pan over the oven and heated to lukewarm. Add yeast and flour and stir until blended. Put in a warm place for 15 minutes. Turn out on a floured board and press to 1 inch thickness. Cut out circles. Fold dough over bits of butter. Place on greased cookie sheet. Let rise 15 minutes and bake 10 minutes in a 350° oven.

BREADS

ZUCCHINI SQUASH BREAD

3 eggs
1 cup of cooking oil
2 cups of sugar
2 cups of peeled and grated zucchini
3 teaspoons of vanilla
3 cups of flour

1 teaspoon of salt
1 teaspoon of soda
3 teaspoons of cinnamon
1/4 teaspoon of baking powder
1/2 cup of chopped nuts

Beat eggs until foamy, add oil, sugar, zucchini, and vanilla. Mix lightly but well, add flour, salt, soda, cinnamon, and baking powder. Mix together. Divide batter in two greased loaf pans. Bake at 325° for one hour or until toothpick comes out clean.

RHUBARB NUT BREAD

1 1/2 cups packed brown sugar
2/3 cup of oil
1 egg
1 cup of sour milk
2 3/4 cups of flour

1 teaspoon of salt
1 teaspoon of baking soda
1 teaspoon of vanilla
1 1/2 cups of diced rhubarb
1/2 cup of nuts

GLAZE:

1/2 cup of sugar
1 teaspoon of butter
1 teaspoon of cinnamon

Mix ingredients in order given. Bake in 2 greased loaf pans at 350° for 45 minutes. Mix the glaze ingredients in a small bowl. Glaze before baking.

HINT: Add 1 tablespoon of vinegar or lemon juice to 1 cup of fresh milk to get sour milk.

BANANA NUT BREAD

1 cup of sugar
2 tablespoons of margarine
1 egg
3 teaspoons of thick, sour milk
1 teaspoon of baking soda

2 cups of flour
1/2 cup of nut meats
1 cup of mashed bananas

Mix sugar, margarine, egg, milk, and soda very well in a large bowl.
Then sift in the flour, nut meats, and bananas. Mix very well. Pour into
a loaf pan and bake at 350° for one hour.

WHOLE WHEAT BATTER BREAD

1 package of dry or compressed yeast
2 tablespoons of honey or brown sugar
1 cup of unsifted whole wheat flour
2 tablespoons of soft shortening

1 1/4 cups of warm water
2 cups of white flour
2 teaspoons of salt

Dissolve yeast in water. Add honey, half the white flour, all the salt
and shortening. Mix very well. Blend in remaining flour with a spoon.
Cover and let rise in a warm place until doubled in size, about 30
minutes. Stir batter down and spread it evenly into a 9X5X3 inch loaf
pan. Let rise in warm place until batter reaches 1/2 inch from top of
pan, about 40 minutes. Bake at 375° for 40-50 minutes. Brush top
with shortening. Makes 1 loaf.

PUMPKIN BREAD

3 cups of flour
1 teaspoon of salt
2 teaspoons of baking powder
3 teaspoons of cinnamon
1/2 cup of nuts

2 cups of pumpkin
4 beaten eggs
1 1/4 cup corn oil
2 cups of sugar

Mix oil, sugar, pumpkin, and eggs well. Blend in dry ingredients. Put in
greased loaf pans and bake 1 hour at 350°. This will stay moist a long
time. Makes two large loaves.

OATMEAL BREAD

2 1/2 cups of boiling water
2 cups of quick cooking oatmeal
1 cup of honey
3/4 cup cooking oil
2 teaspoons of salt
4 beaten eggs
2 small packages of yeast
2 cups of whole wheat flour

Dissolve yeast in 1 cup of water. In a separate bowl, pour boiling water over oatmeal and cool to lukewarm. Then beat the rest of ingredients together in the oatmeal bowl. Add yeast, make sure the mixture isn't too warm. Add enough flour to make a spongy dough that is not sticky. Grease top and let rise. Put in a loaf pan. Bake at 400° for 10 minutes. Turn to 350° for 25-30 minutes.

SUSAN'S WHOLE WHEAT BREAD

1 cup of milk
1 tablespoon of salt
3 tablespoons of butter
4 tablespoons of honey or maple syrup
1 cake of yeast
1 cup of warm water
2 cups of sifted flour
4 cups of whole wheat flour

Scald milk. Add salt, syrup, and 3/4 cup of warm water. Stir well. Let cool to lukewarm. In remaining 1/4 cup of water dissolve the yeast; add to other mixture. Add flours gradually and knead into a smooth ball. Place in buttered bowl and brush top with soft butter. Let rise until double. Knead lightly and shape into a loaf and place into a pan. Brush with soft butter and let rise to double. Bake at 350° for 50-60 minutes.

COBLENTZ'S HABITS

As we went to church services this morning, is it just a habit of going? Well, most people go to church on Sunday and some have the habit of going to church at other times. If anyone tells you religion is just a habit - we'd answer them: it is better to have that habit than not to have it at all.

As a family, you automatically get in the same habit. Especially in our adult life, habits are what cause us to live a "structured" life. We get up at the same time each morning. Some are going out to milk the cows, some are getting breakfast, and some are getting their lunch buckets packed for lunch while at work. The list could go on and on, what takes place in the early morning hours. It, anyways, seems it's a hustle and bustle, or should I say, it's a habit of doing it. It seems we eat much the same food for breakfast, dinner, and supper.

We get dressed, wash, and comb our hair and off to work we go - all without specific pre-planning. The average person gets to work, they do their job.

We then have a tendency to spend money after we get our weekly pay checks for things we could do without, when actually it's just a plain old habit. It's just this kind of habit that is hard to change.

MY WHOLE WHEAT BREAD

1 package of yeast
1/4 cup of lukewarm water
2 tablespoons of sugar
1 tablespoon of salt
3 1/4 cups of sifted whole wheat flour

2 tablespoons of cooking oil
2 cups of milk, scalded
2 1/4 cups of white flour
1 teaspoon of sugar

Put yeast into lukewarm water, add 1 teaspoon of sugar. Stir well. Let stand in warm place until foamy. Pour milk into separate mixing bowl; add remaining sugar and salt. Cool until lukewarm. Add yeast. Add 3 cups of whole wheat flour (enough to make a soft dough); beat thoroughly. Add shortening. Let dough stand for 10 minutes, working in remaining whole wheat flour, until dough is soft, but not sticky. Place in a bowl and let rise. Knead. Shape into loaves. Let rise until double. Bake in hot oven at 400° for 10 minutes. Then reduce heat to 375° and bake 40 minutes. Makes 2 loaves.

GRANDMA'S CINNARAISIN BREAD

1 cup of brown sugar
1/2 cup of water
1 cup of raisins
2 1/2 teaspoons of baking powder
1 1/2 teaspoons of cinnamon
1 teaspoon salt

2 tablespoons of melted butter
1 egg
2 1/2 cups of sifted flour
1/2 cup of milk

Butter a 9X5X3 inch loaf pan. Combine brown sugar and water in small saucepan. Bring it to a boil. Add raisins and set aside to completely cool. Into a large bowl, sift together flour, baking powder, cinnamon, and salt. In small bowl, beat together milk, egg, and butter; stir in cooled raisin mixture. Add liquid ingredients to dry ingredients and stir until completely blended. Gently pour into the prepared pan. Bake 1 hour at 375° or until toothpick inserted in center comes out clean. Cool in pan for 10 minutes. Remove bread from pan and cool.

GARDEN RHUBARB BREAD

1 1/2 cups of brown sugar
2/3 cup of oil
1 egg
1 cup of sour milk
2 3/4 cups of flour

1 teaspoon of salt
1 teaspoon of baking soda
1 teaspoon of vanilla
1 1/2 cups of diced, rhubarb

GLAZE:
1/2 cup of sugar
1 teaspoon of butter
1 teaspoon of cinnamon

Mix ingredients in order given. Bake in 2 greased loaf pans at 350° for 45 minutes. Brush on glaze and let bread cool.

APPLE BREAD

1 cup of sugar
1/2 cup of shortening
2 eggs
1 teaspoon of vanilla
1/4 teaspoon of cinnamon

2 cups of self-rising flour
2 cups of chopped, pared apples
1 tablespoon of sugar

Heat oven to 350°. Grease and flour a 9X5X3 inch loaf pan. Mix 1 cup of sugar, shortening, eggs, and vanilla. Stir in flour until smooth, stir in apples and nuts. Spread in a pan. Mix 1 tablespoon of sugar and cinnamon. Sprinkle over batter. Bake until wooden toothpick comes out clean (about an hour). Remove from pan immediately. Let set before slicing. Makes one loaf.

HOBO BREAD

1 cup of raisins

2 teaspoons of baking soda

1 cup of boiling water

2 tablespoons of vegetable oil

1 cup of brown sugar

1/2 teaspoon of salt

Mix raisins, soda, and boiling water. Cover and let stand overnight or until cooled. When cool, add dry ingredients and oil. Mix well. Pour into small loaf pan. Bake at 350° for one hour. Makes one small loaf.

CORN BREAD

1 cup of corn meal

1 cup of flour

1/4 cup of sugar

1/2 teaspoon of salt

4 teaspoons of baking powder

1 egg

1 cup of milk

1/4 cup of soft shortening

Stir together and bake in a pan for 25 to 30 minutes at about 350°

BEN'S FAVORITE COFFEECAKE

3 cups of flour

2 cups of sugar

1/2 teaspoon of nutmeg

1/2 teaspoon of cinnamon

2 teaspoons of baking soda

1/2 teaspoon of salt

1/4 cup of shortening

1/2 teaspoon of crushed cloves

2 cups of buttermilk

Mix together the first six ingredients. Then add the shortening, To the rest, add buttermilk with soda. Blend well. Pour into greased and floured 9X13X2 inch pan. Bake at 350° for 30 minutes or until done. Add your own icing.

SPEEDY ROLLS

1/2 cup of sugar
2 packages of yeast
6 1/2 cups of flour
2 eggs
1/3 cup of shortening or butter
1 tablespoon of salt
2 cups of lukewarm water

Place water, sugar, salt, yeast, and 2 cups of flour in a bowl. Beat 2 minutes. Add eggs and shortening and beat 1 minute. Gradually add 4 1/2 cups of flour, stir until firm. Allow dough to set at least 20 minutes for easy handling. Then roll out and spread with melted butter. Sprinkle with brown sugar and cinnamon. Roll up like a jelly roll and slice vertically. Put in greased pans and let rise. Bake at 375° for 25 to 30 minutes or until done.

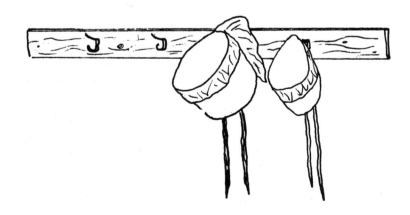

HOMEMADE BREAD

1 package of yeast
2 1/2 cups of lukewarm water
1 tablespoon of salt
2 tablespoons of sugar
lard (amount the size of an egg)
Enough flour to make a soft dough

Mix ingredients and let rise till double. Punch down. Let rise again.
Work down and form loaves. Put in greased loaf pans. Bake in a 325°
oven around 1/2 hour.

*BREAD MEMORIES - As a young girl at home with my parents, my mother taught
me how to bake bread. The aroma of loaves of bread lifted from the oven made a
good smell throughout the house. We would take it from the oven, slice it, and
smear it with butter. Yummy!*

THE BASICS OF BAKING BREAD

1. Make sure the milk or water being used in a bread recipe
is lukewarm.

2. Store dough in a warm place, away from drafts, to rise.
Make sure you keep it covered with a loose piece of
cheesecloth or plastic wrap.

3. When removing the bread from the oven, brush the top
with butter or margarine. This will make for a softer crust.
Sealing the bread in a plastic bag before it is cool will keep
the bread fresh.

AMISH FRIENDSHIP BREAD

Although the origin of this recipe is uncertain, it is a favorite among readers of The Amish Cook. It is the single most requested recipe in the reader mail. So for the benefit of the curious, here is that much sought-after bread recipe:

PART I

Instructions for the sourdough starter:

3 1/2 cups of bread flour
1 tablespoon of sugar
1 package of dry, active yeast
2 cups of warm water

Combine flour, sugar, and undissolved yeast into a large bowl. Gradually add warm water to dry ingredients. Beat until smooth. Cover with transparent wrap and let stand in a warm place for two days.

PART II

1 cup of starter
1 cup of flour   1 1/2 teaspoons of baking powder
1 cup of sugar   3 eggs
1 cup of milk   2 teaspoons of cinnamon
1 cup of flour   1 teaspoon of vanilla
1 cup of sugar   1/2 teaspoon of salt
1 cup of milk   1/2 teaspoon of soda
2/3 cup of oil   1 large box of vanilla instant pudding
2 cups of flour   1 cup of chopped nuts (optional)
1/2 cups of sugar

Put one cup of starter in a bowl. Keep the rest in your refrigerator. The starter will keep for a long time.

Directions:

Day 1: Do nothing to the one cup of starter.
Day 2,3,4: Stir starter with a wooden spoon
Day 5: Add one cup of flour, 1 cup of sugar, 1 cup of milk. Stir with wooden spoon. Re-cover the mixture and set in a warm place.
Day 6,7,8,9: Stir with a wooden spoon and re-cover.
Day 10: Add 1 cup of flour, 1 cup of sugar, 1 cup of milk, stir. Divide into three containers (1 cup each) and give to three friends with these instructions:

To remainder: add 2/3 cup of oil, 2 cups of flour, 3 eggs, 2 teaspoons of cinnamon, 1 teaspoons of vanilla, 1/2 teaspoon of salt, and 1/2 teaspoon of soda. Add one large box of instant vanilla pudding mix and one cup of nuts. Pour into two well-greased and floured loaf pans and bake 40 to 50 minutes at 350°. Watch towards the end of baking time and cover with foil to prevent burning. Also, test for doneness with a toothpick so it does not get too well done. Cool in pans for 10 minutes and then remove.

Do not use a metal spoon. Do not refrigerate. Cover loosely. You can also bake this in a bundt pan. The leftover starter can be used for future sourdough recipes.

RAISIN BRAN MUFFINS

1 1/4 cups of milk
1 1/2 cups of raisin bran cereal
1 1/2 cups of flour
1/3 cup of sugar
1 teaspoon of salt
3 teaspoons of baking powder
1 egg, beaten
1/4 cup of melted shortening

Combine milk and cereal in a large bowl. Mix flour with sugar, salt, and baking powder. Add egg and melted shortening to milk and cereal. Add dry ingredients. Mix until dry ingredients are moistened. Batter will be lumpy, not smooth. Fill greased muffin pan cups 2/3 full. Bake in a 400° oven 20 to 25 minutes. Makes 12 medium-sized muffins.

MORNING MUFFINS

5 teaspoons of shortening (can be part butter)
1/2 cup sugar
1 egg yolk
1 cup of flour
1/4 teaspoon of salt
2 teaspoons of baking powder
1/4 teaspoon of nutmeg
1/2 cup of milk
egg white

Rolling Mixture: 1/2 teaspoon of cinnamon, 1/2 cup of sugar

Mix sugar and shortening. Gradually add 1/2 cup of sugar. Blend in one egg yolk. Next add flour, salt, baking powder, nutmeg, and milk. Then fold in egg white. Bake in greased muffin cups. Fill cups 1/2 full. Bake for 20-25 minutes at 350°. Immediately roll muffins in melted butter, then in mixture of 1/2 cup of sugar and teaspoon of cinnamon. Serve warm. Makes a dozen muffins.

LOVINA'S BEST CORN BREAD

2 eggs
1 cup of milk
1/4 cup of melted shortening
3/4 cup of yellow corn meal
1 cup of flour
1 teaspoon of salt
3 teaspoons of baking powder
2 tablespoons of sugar

Beat all ingredients until smooth. Bake in a waxed paper lined 9 inch square pan at 400°, about 20 minutes.

MIDWESTERN RAISIN BREAD

1 1/2 cups of milk
1/4 cup of sugar
2 teaspoons of salt
1/2 cup of butter
1 cup of unseasoned mashed potatoes
1/2 cup of warm water
2 packages of yeast
7 1/2 cups of flour
1 1/2 cups of raisins

Filling: 1/2 cup of sugar, 2 teaspoons of cinnamon, 1/2 cup of melted butter or oleo.

Scald the milk. Remove from flame and add sugar, salt, butter, and mashed potatoes. Cool. Dissolve yeast in the warm water in a separate bowl. Then add to the milk mixture. Add raisins and flour. Let it rise in a nice, warm place for 1 1/2 hours. Divide dough in 2 loaves. Roll out on a board and spread half of the filling on each roll. Roll up as for jelly roll and pinch edges together and bake in loaf pans at 350° to 375° for 45 minutes.

NANCY'S COFFEE CAKE

3/4 cup warm water
1 package of yeast
1 egg
1/4 cup of sugar
1/4 cup of lard
1 teaspoon of salt
2 1/4 cups of flour

Topping: margarine, cinnamon, and brown sugar.

Dissolve yeast in water. Add sugar, salt, and half of the flour. Beat in the egg. Add lard, beat in rest of flour until the mixture is smooth. Drop by spoon in an oblong loaf pan. Let rise in warm place till double. Bake 30 minutes at 375°. Mix topping ingredients and rub on top of the cake.

RUSHY ROLLS

3/4 cup of warm water
1/4 cup of sugar
2 1/4 cups of sifted bread flour
1/4 cup of soft shortening or butter
1 package or tablespoon of dry yeast
1 teaspoon of salt
1 egg

Dissolve yeast in water, add sugar, salt, and about half the flour. Beat thoroughly for a couple of minutes. Add egg and shortening. Then gradually beat in the remaining flour until smooth. Bake for 10 minutes at 350°. Makes 1 dozen.

LONG JOHN ROLLS

2 packages of dry yeast
1 cup of lukewarm water
1 cup of lukewarm milk
1/2 cup of margarine
2/3 cup of sugar

2 eggs
1/2 teaspoon of salt
1/8 teaspoon of nutmeg
6 or 7 cups of flour

Dissolve yeast into lukewarm water. Scald milk and let stand to cool, then blend together margarine, sugar, and well-beaten eggs. Put in nutmeg. Put the milk in the yeast and water and add 3 cups of flour (until it is easy to handle). Put in warm place; let rise till double. Roll out and cut into oblong pieces. Let rise again. Fry in deep fat. Frosting may be added if desired. Makes 3 dozen.

CARAMEL PECAN CINNAMON ROLLS

1/4 cup of shortening
1/2 cup of sugar
1 package of yeast
1 teaspoon of salt

5-6 cups of flour
2 eggs
1 1/2 cups of scalded milk

Mix and let rise for one hour.

Topping: Melt together 1 1/2 cups of brown sugar, 6 tablespoons of oleo, 4 tablespoons of corn syrup, and a teaspoon of vanilla. Spread in the bottom of two 9X13 pans and sprinkle with pecans. Place rolls on top of the mixture and bake at 425° for 15-20 minutes. Turn upside down on sheets and remove from pans.

LARD CAKES

We serve these on butchering hog day to our helpers.

1 1/2 cups of cream
2 1/4 cups of sour milk
2 heaping teaspoons of baking soda
3 eggs

Mix together and add flour, enough to match a pie dough. Add a little salt and sugar if you wish. Roll out and cut-up in any shape as big as you wish. Cut a slit into the center of the dough. Then drop them into a kettle of hot lard. Drain and roll in a pan of sugar. Eat fresh, they get stale quickly.

AMISH DOUGHNUTS

5 cups of milk
5 tablespoons of yeast
1 1/4 cups of shortening
1 1/4 cups of sugar

5 teaspoons of salt
5 eggs, beaten
17 1/2 cups of flour
1 1/4 cups of warm water

Scald 5 cups of milk. Let cool slightly. Dissolve 5 tablespoons of yeast in 1 1/4 cups of warm water. Add to milk. Stir in 7 1/2 cups of flour. Beat, cover and let rise in warm place till double in size. Cream shortening, sugar, salt, and eggs. Add to yeast mixture, then add 10 cups of flour. Knead. Let rise till double in size. Knead. Roll out to 1/4 to 1/2 inch thick. Cut with cutter. Let rise till double in size. Fry in a hot kettle of oil. Roll in sugar.

DOUGHNUT FROSTING

1/4 cup of margarine
1/4 teaspoon of salt
1/3 cup of maple syrup

2 teaspoons of vanilla
3 cups of confectioners sugar
3 tablespoons of milk

Mix until smooth and creamy. Spread on doughnuts.

AUNT ELIZABETH'S YEAST DOUGHNUTS

2 cakes of yeast
1 cup of lukewarm water
1 cup of scalded milk
6 cups of flour

2 teaspoons of salt
1/4 pound of shortening
3 eggs
4 tablespoons of sugar

Sift flour. In a separate bowl, pour water over yeast and 1 tablespoon of sugar. Stir and let stand.

Meanwhile, pour scalded milk in a bowl and add salt, 3 tablespoons of sugar, and then shortening. When lukewarm, add water and yeast and 3 cups of flour. Beat until smooth and add beaten eggs and rest of flour. Let rise until double. Punch down. Cut out into doughnut shapes and let rise again. Then fry in hot grease until golden.

AUNT EICHER'S CREAM STICKS

2 packages of yeast, dissolved in 1 cup of warm water.
1 cup of milk, scalded
2/3 cup of sugar
1/2 teaspoon of salt
6 cups of flour
1/2 cup of oleo
2 eggs
1 teaspoon of vanilla

Frosting: 1/2 cup of brown sugar, 2 tablespoons of milk, 4 tablespoons of butter. Mix and spread over sticks.

Let dough rise until double in size. Knead and then form dough into sticks 3 1/2 X 1 1/2 inches. Let rise again. Deep fry in fat. Remove when golden.

SUNDAYS

It's Sunday!

We attend church services at 9 a.m. Church is held in the home of a congregation member. Services usually last until 11:30 a.m. or noon. In the summertime church is mostly held in well-cleaned tool sheds or in the driveway of the barn. In the wintertime, the services are held in the houses. It is lots nicer in the summertime.

The churches are divided into districts and most churches have from twenty to thirty families in a district. There is a bishop, two ministers, and a deacon in each church district.

Before church services, cookies and crackers or some other treat is passed around to the small children. They look forward to it.

After church, a lunch-type meal is served to all those who attended. The lunch consists of coffee (some also serve tea), bologna or ham, cheese or homemade cheese spread, bread, a peanut butter and marshmallow creme mixture, red beets, apple butter, and some have lettuce. The menu varies from place to place.

In the afternoon, visiting takes place and most leave for home. Some return for the evening meal. We had 179 once for the evening meal after we had church at our house. That was the most we ever had. I didn't realize there would be that many people coming, but we had plenty to feed them all. The desserts almost ran out, but we had to peel more potatoes for mashed potatoes and cook more noodles for chicken noodles. Vegetables were opened jar by jar. If you've got plenty - no worry. Lots of work, though!

By the way, the young unmarried girls help serve the meals at dinnertime.

PIES, CAKES, COOKIES

and other delicious desserts!

CHAPTER 4

LEAH'S CINNAMON PUDDING

Step 1:
2 cups of brown sugar
2 tablespoons of margarine
1 1/2 cups of cold water
Mix and let come to a boil.

Step 2:
1 cup of white sugar
2 tablespoons of margarine
1 cup of milk
2 teaspoons of cinnamon
2 teaspoons of baking powder, enough flour to make a batter.
Mix thoroughly.

Put step 2 in bottom of a greased pan. Pour Step 1 over it and sprinkle with nuts if you wish. Bake 45 minutes at 350°. Serve with whipped cream.

CHERRY COBBLER

1 cup of sifted flour
2 teaspoons of baking powder
1/8 teaspoon of salt
1/4 cup of butter

1 cup of sugar
1/2 cup of milk
1 can of pitted sour cherries

Sift flour, baking powder, salt, and water. Mix well and add milk and melted butter. Pour into a greased pan. Add cherries and bake in 375° oven for 1 hour.

QUILTING BEES

A quilting bee is an enjoyable day!

There are sometimes one, two, three, and even four quilts put in quilting frames, which have been marked off with some kind of a design. How many quilts are put in frame, depends on how many women are invited.

For two quilts, around 40 women are invited, as there is always someone who can't be present. The women gather around the frame and the stitching (and the gossip!) begins. News about their children, gardens, relatives, and you-name-it begins to fill the room.

In the forenoon, treats are passed around to all. A variety of cookies and coffee is usually served.

At noon, a delicious meal is served to all and then they return to the quilts to stitch some more. Treats are again passed around in the afternoon. Lots of singing and yodeling also takes place at a quilting bee.

Wonder how many stitches are on a quilt like that till its completed? I suppose it would be remarkable to know!

It's a lot of work to have a quilting bee. You buy the material for the quilt, then needles and thread. You sew the material together (the length and width you prefer). Then you mark it off to some kind of design and then it's ready to be put in a quilting frame.

CHOCOLATE CHIP BROWNIES

2 cups of brown sugar
pinch of salt
1/2 cup of butter
1 teaspoon of vanilla
2 eggs

2 cups of flour
1 teaspoon of baking powder
1 cup of chocolate chips
1/2 teaspoon of baking soda

Pour sugar into a mixing bowl. Melt butter and pour over sugar. Mix well. Add eggs and mix. Add flour and dry ingredients. Spread in buttered pan. Sprinkle chips on top, bake at about 350° until lightly browned. Butterscotch chips are also good with this.

TAPIOCA PUDDING

2 cups of tapioca
2 quarts of water
6 ounce package of Jello (any flavor, I usually use strawberry)
3 cups of sugar

Cook tapioca and water for 10 minutes. Remove from stove. Add sugar and Jello and stir well. Let get cold and set. If too thick, add water. Stir a few times while cooking, as tapioca will settle to the bottom. Whip 1 can of Rich's topping until it is very stiff. Add the amount of tapioca you desire. Mix very well.

MINUTE TAPIOCA PUDDING

1 egg, slightly beaten
1/3 cup of sugar
1/8 teaspoon of salt
3/4 teaspoon of vanilla

2 3/4 cups of milk
3 tablespoons of tapioca

In a saucepan, mix all ingredients except vanilla. Let stand five minutes. Cook over medium heat, stirring constantly until mixture comes to a full boil, about 6-8 minutes. Pudding will thicken as it cools. Remove from heat. Stir in vanilla. Stir once after 20 minutes. Serve warm or cold. Makes 5 servings.

PLUM PUDDING

2 packages of butterscotch pudding
1 pound of pitted prunes
1 package of graham crackers
2 cups of English walnuts
4 cups of mini-marshmallows

Prepare pudding as directed on package. Cool. Put prunes in enough water to cover, and place in a covered saucepan. Bring to a boil, then remove from heat and cool without removing lid. Crush graham crackers and put 3/4 of the crumbs in the bottom of a large oblong dish. Reserve 1/4 of the crumbs. On top of crumbs, layer the prunes, marshmallows, nuts, and pudding. Top with remaining crushed graham cracker crumbs. Chill and serve.

BREAD PUDDING

4 cups of bread cubes	dash of salt
1 quart of hot milk	1 cup of sugar
3 tablespoons of butter	1/2 teaspoon of vanilla
4 eggs, separated	

Boil the milk. After it is has been boiled, combine it with bread cubes and butter. Then allow it to stand for 10 minutes. In a separate bowl, beat egg yolks and salt until fluffy. Add sugar and vanilla to the yolks, beat until lemon colored. Add bread mixture. Pour into a greased 2 quart baking dish and bake at 350° for 50 minutes.

DATE-NUT PUDDING

1 package of dates
1 teaspoon of baking soda
1 cup of boiling water
4 tablespoons of shortening
1 cup of sugar

1 egg
1 2/3 cup of flour
1/2 teaspoon of salt
1 teaspoon of vanilla
1/2 cup of nuts

Pit and quarter dates, place in a bowl. Add baking soda and pour boiling water over the dates. Let cool. Cream shortening and add sugar and egg. Beat. Add flour and salt alternately to the date mixture. Stir in vanilla and nuts. Pour into a greased and flour pan. Bake 40 minutes at 350°. Top with whipped cream. Serve cool.

PUMPKIN BARS

2 cups of flour
2 teaspoons of baking powder
1/2 teaspoon of salt
2 teaspoons of cinnamon
4 eggs

1 cup of walnuts
2 cups of pumpkin
1 teaspoon of baking soda
2 cups of sugar
1 cup of oil

Mix all of the above ingredients very well. Shape into bars. Put on a large cookie sheet that has been greased and floured. Bake at 350° for 25-30 minutes. Ice with cream cheese icing:

Cream Cheese Icing:

1/2 stick of oleo
8 ounces of cream cheese

1 box of powdered sugar
1 teaspoon of vanilla

Mix very well. Ice bars after they cool.

RHUBARB BUTTER CRUNCH

3 cups of rhubarb   3 tablespoons of flour
1 cup of sugar

Topping: 1 cup of brown sugar, 1 cup of raw rolled oats, 1 1/2 cups of flour, 1/4 cup of butter or shortening.

Mix rhubarb, sugar, and flour well and place in a greased baking dish. Combine the topping ingredients and sprinkle it over the rhubarb mixture. Bake at 370° for 40 minutes. Serve warm with milk or cream.

CHERRY CRUNCH

1 package of white cake mix
1 stick of oleo
2 cans of cherry pie filling

Put pie filling in a greased 9X13 inch pan. Crumble cake mix and oleo together. Spread over the top of pie filling and bake at 375° for 25-30 minutes. Serve with whipped cream while warm.

SODA CRACKER DELIGHT

6 egg whites
2 cups of white sugar

Beat until stiff. Fold in:

1 1/2 cups of soda crackers, crumbled
1 cup of nuts
1 tablespoon of vanilla

Bake in ungreased pan at 350° until golden brown. Mix together 2 pints of Dream Whip™ and a can of crushed, drained pineapples and pour over the cooked product.

LOVINA'S CHOCOLATE MOUSSE

1 quart soft vanilla ice cream
1 large package of instant chocolate pudding
1 1/2 cups of cold milk
1/2 bag of chocolate chips
1 medium container Cool Whip

Ritz Crackers™
3/4 cup of butter

Crush 55 Ritz crackers. Melt the margarine. Mix crackers and margarine and bake at 320° for 10 minutes in a 13X9 inch pan. Mix instant pudding with milk. Add soft ice cream until smooth. Gently spread over cooled crust. Spread Cool Whip on top. Sprinkle with Heath™ bits. Set chill overnight.

INDIANA HEAVENLY STRAWBERRY DESSERT

1 box (3 ounces) strawberry Jello
1 1/4 cup of undrained strawberries, mashed and sugared
1 tablespoon of sugar
1/2 pint of whipped cream
pinch of salt
1 angel food cake
1 1/4 cup of boiling water

Dissolve Jello in water. Stir in berries, sugar, and salt. Refrigerate until it begins to thicken. Whip cream and fold Jello into the mixture. Tear cake into pieces and put in 13X9 inch pan. Pour strawberry mixture over the cake and refrigerate.

DOLLIES

1 stick of margarine or oleo
1 1/2 cups of graham cracker crumbs
1 1/2 cups of chocolate chips
1 1/2 cups of flaked coconut
15 ounces of sweetened condensed milk

1 cup of chopped nuts

Melt butter in 13X9X2 inch pan. Sprinkle crumbs, coconut, chocolate chips, and nuts on top of the butter. Pour milk over all. Bake at 350° for 30 minutes. Cool and cut into squares.

HEAVENLY BITS

2 sticks of oleo
6 heaping tablespoons of powdered sugar
1 tablespoon of vanilla
1 tablespoon of water
2 1/2 cups of flour

Mix and then drop by teaspoon onto a greased and floured cookie sheet. Bake at 350° for 15 to 20 minutes. Roll in powdered sugar while still warm.

SOFT PRETZELS

2 packages of yeast
2 cups of warm water
1 teaspoon of salt

5 cups of flour
2 teaspoons of baking soda
salt

Let yeast dissolve in 1 1/2 cups of room temperature water. Then stir in salt and flour. Knead until the texture is soft and smooth. Let rise 20 minutes. Separate the dough into 18 pieces. Roll each piece into narrow broomstick shaped rolls and then sculpt into a pretzel shape. Dissolve your baking soda in 1/2 cup of warm water. Dip each pretzel into the soda-water mix. Add salt and cook for 20 minutes at 425°.

COOKIES

MONSTER COOKIES

12 eggs
4 cups of brown sugar
4 cups of white sugar
1 tablespoon of vanilla
1 tablespoon of clear corn syrup
8 teaspoons of baking soda
1 pound of butter or oleo
3 pounds of peanut butter (plain or crunchy)
18 cups of oatmeal
1 pound of chocolate chips
1 pound of M & Ms™

Mix in order given in a big bowl until smooth. Drop by spoonfuls on greased cookie sheet. Bake at 350° about 12 minutes. Do not overbake.

QUAKER COOKIES

1 cup of margarine
2 cups of brown sugar
2 eggs
2 teaspoons of vanilla
1 1/2 teaspoons of baking soda
1 teaspoon of salt
2 1/4 cups of flour
3 cups of rolled oats
white sugar

Cream margarine and sugar. Add eggs and vanilla. Mix well. Add flour, salt, and soda. Add rolled oats last. Stir until you get a nice, smooth batter.

Chill dough, then make into balls the size of a walnut. Roll in white sugar. Bake 10-15 minutes at 350°.

MARLENE'S NO-BAKE COOKIES

1/2 cup of margarine
1 teaspoon of vanilla
1 egg
1/2 cup of nuts
4 cups of Rice Krispies™

3/4 cup of white sugar
eight ounces of cut dates

Cook egg, sugar, margarine, and dates over a low heat for 10 minutes. Cool slightly and stir in vanilla, Rice Krispies, and nuts. Make into balls. Refrigerate overnight.

NO-BAKE CHOCOLATE COOKIES

1/3 cup of cocoa
2 cups of sugar
1/2 cup of butter
1/2 cup of milk

2 1/2 cups of rolled oats
1/2 cup of peanut butter
1 teaspoon of vanilla

Mix together butter, cocoa, sugar, and milk and boil for 3 minutes. Take off heat, then add oats and peanut butter and vanilla. Stir well. Before it cools, form into cookies by dropping by teaspoon onto waxed paper. Let cool. Then ready to eat. Store in a container at room temperature.

LANCASTER COUNTY MOLASSES COOKIES

5 cups of sugar
2 1/2 cups of lard
4 eggs
1 cup of molasses
3 tablespoons of baking soda

1 teaspoon of baking powder
1 teaspoon of salt
2 teaspoons of vanilla
12-15 cups of flour
1 cup of hot water

Cream first 4 ingredients. Dissolve soda, baking powder and salt in hot water. Add to creamy mixture. Add vanilla and flour. Mix very well. It will be very thick, and difficult to mix. Make into small balls and bake on greased cookie sheet at 350°.

GERMAN ICE-BOX OATMEAL COOKIES

1 cup of lard

1 cup of brown sugar

1 cup of white sugar

2 beaten eggs

1 teaspoon of vanilla

1 1/2 cups of flour

1 teaspoon of baking soda

1 teaspoon of salt

3 cups of oatmeal

1/2 cup of nuts (optional)

Cream together lard and sugars. Add beaten eggs and vanilla. Sift together flour, baking soda, and salt and add to the sugar mixture. Then add the oatmeal and nuts. Mix well. Shape the mixture into 2 or 3 long rolls. Chill overnight. Slice and bake at 350° until done - about 10 minutes. Slices rolls vertically, each slice should be 1/2 inch thick.

SQUASH COOKIES

1 cup of lard

2 cups of squash or pumpkin

2 cups of sugar

4 1/2 cups of flour

2 teaspoons of baking soda

2 teaspoons of cinnamon

2 teaspoons of baking powder

dates, nuts or raisins (optional)

Cream together lard, squash, and sugar. Add dry ingredients. Stir together well and drop by teaspoon onto a lightly greased cookie sheet. Bake at 350° until done.

CHRISTMAS COOKIES

3 cups of flour

1 cup of sugar

1 teaspoon of baking soda

1/2 teaspoon of salt

1 1/4 cups of margarine

3 tablespoons of milk

2 eggs

1 teaspoon of cream of tartar

1 teaspoon of vanilla

Mix dry ingredients. Add remaining ingredients and stir until you get a soft dough. Roll out thinly. Cut in any shape desired. Bake at 375° for about 10 minutes, or until golden around the edges. Let cool and decorate as you wish.

OATMEAL WHOOPIE PIE COOKIES

2 cups of brown sugar
3/4 cup of butter
2 eggs
1/2 teaspoon of salt
2 cups of flour

2 cups of oatmeal
1 teaspoon of cinnamon
2 teaspoons of baking soda
1 teaspoon of baking powder
3 tablespoons of boiling water

Cream butter, sugar, and eggs. Sift together flour, salt, and baking powder and add to creamed mixture. Add cinnamon and oatmeal. Mix well. Add soda to hot water and add to batter. Mix well.

Drop by tablespoon onto greased cookie sheet; bake 10-15 minutes in 325° oven.

Filling:

1 egg white
1 tablespoon of vanilla
2 tablespoons of milk

2 cups of powdered sugar
1/4 cup of shortening

Combine egg white, vanilla, milk, and 1 cup of powdered sugar. Cream well. Add rest of ingredients and beat. Put filling between 2 cookies. Wrap each whoopie pie cookie in plastic wrap.

AFTER-CHURCH CHOCOLATE CHIP COOKIES

2 cups of butter
2 cups of white sugar
2 teaspoons of hot water
2 teaspoons of vanilla
1-12 ounce package of chocolate chips

4 beaten eggs
5 cups of flour
2 cups of brown sugar
2 teaspoons of baking soda

Cream shortening and sugars. Add beaten eggs. Dissolve soda in hot water. Mix alternately with flour sifted with salt, add chocolate chips. Flavor with vanilla. Stir well. Drop by teaspoon onto greased cookie sheets. Bake 10 to 12 minutes at 375°.

BROOMSTICK COOKIES

3 cups of brown sugar
1 1/2 cups of shortening
1 cup of dark corn syrup
3 eggs
3/4 cup of raisins (cover with water and cook until plump)

2 teaspoons of vanilla
1/2 cup of milk
6 1/2 - 7 cups of flour

Mix all ingredients to consistency of pie dough. Roll in hand to form broomsticks. Place lengthwise on a cookie sheet. Bake at 375° for 15 to 20 minutes. Let stand a few minutes and top with powdered sugar. Cut diagonally.

AUNT ZOOK'S SUGAR COOKIES

1 cup of vegetable oil
1 cup of butter
1 cup of powdered sugar
1 cup of sugar
2 eggs
1/2 teaspoon of cream of tartar

1/2 teaspoon of soda
1/2 teaspoon of salt
1 teaspoon of vanilla
5 1/4 cups of flour

Mix everything very well. Roll into 1 inch balls and press flat with the bottom of a glass dipped in sugar. Bake at 350° for 10-12 minutes.

PEANUT BUTTER COOKIES

1 cup of shortening
2 eggs
1/2 teaspoon of baking soda
1 1/2 cups of white sugar

1 teaspoon of vanilla
2 1/2 cups of flour
1 cup of peanut butter
1/2 teaspoon of salt

Mix the above ingredients until smooth. Drop by teaspoon onto a cookie sheet. Bake at 370° for 12 minutes. Makes 50 cookies.

TOLD-YOU-SO COOKIES

1 cup of shortening
3/4 cup of brown sugar
3/4 cup of white sugar
2 beaten eggs
1 teaspoon of hot water

1 teaspoon of vanilla

Sift the above ingredients together and add:

1 1/2 cups of sifted flour
1 teaspoon of salt
1 teaspoon of soda

Stir well. Add the following ingredients:

2 cups of oatmeal
1 cup of chopped nuts
1 package of chocolate chips.

Stir well. Drop by teaspoon onto a cookie sheet. Bake at 350° for 10-15 minutes.

RANGER COOKIES

1 cup of brown sugar
1 cup of sugar
1 cup of lard
2 eggs
1 tablespoon of vanilla
1/2 teaspoon of salt

1/2 teaspoon of baking soda
1 teaspoon of baking powder
2 cups of flour
2 cups of Rice Krispies
2 cups of rolled oats

Cream first 3 ingredients. Add beaten eggs and vanilla, mix thoroughly. Add sifted, dry ingredients. Stir in cereal. Roll batter into walnut size balls or drop scant tablespoon on ungreased cookie sheet. Bake 10 minutes at 400°. Makes 5 to 6 dozen, a crunchy cookie.

CRYBABY COOKIES

3/4 cup of shortening
1 cup of sugar
2 eggs, beaten
1 cup of light molasses
4 cups of flour
3/4 cup of strong, cold coffee

1 teaspoon of salt
1 teaspoon of baking soda
2 teaspoons of cinnamon
2 teaspoons of ginger
1/2 teaspoon of cloves

Mix all together. Drop by teaspoon onto a greased cookie sheet. Bake at 350° for 10-15 minutes. Makes about 7 dozen.

PINWHEEL COOKIES

1/2 cup of butter or lard
1 1/2 cups of flour
1/8 teaspoon of salt
3 tablespoons of milk
1/2 teaspoon vanilla

1/2 cup of sugar
1 egg yolk
1 1/2 teaspoons of baking soda
1 1/2 teaspoon cocoa

Mix well (except cocoa and vanilla). Divide dough into two parts. To one part, add 1 1/2 teaspoons of cocoa. Into the other part, add 1/2 teaspoon of vanilla and roll white dough into a thin, rectangular sheet, the roll cocoa dough the same. Place the white dough on the cocoa dough and press together. Roll as for a jelly roll - a tight roll, 2 inches in diameter. Set in the icebox or out to chill overnight. In the morning, cut in 1/4 inch slices and arrange flat in a pan or on a cookie sheet and bake at 350° until done - about 10 minutes.

HAYSTACK COOKIES

1-12 ounce package of butterscotch bits
1-5 ounce can of chow mein noodles
2 cups of unsalted peanuts

Melt butterscotch bits in a double boiler. Add remaining ingredients. Mix well. Drop onto cookie sheet. Cool. Delicious cookies!

YODER'S COOKIES

2 cups of sugar
1 cup of lard
2 eggs
1 cup of sour milk
1 teaspoon of vanilla

2 teaspoons of baking soda
1/2 teaspoon of cream of tartar
1/2 teaspoon of nutmeg
4 cups of flour

Cream sugar and shortening. Add eggs and beat well. Add flour, nutmeg, cream of tartar, and vanilla. Mix very well. Drop mixture by teaspoon onto a lightly greased cookie sheet. Cook for 12-15 minutes at 375° until browned. Makes 36 cookies.

ANGEL COOKIES

1/2 cup of butter
1/2 cup of shortening
1/2 cup of brown sugar
1/2 cup of white sugar
1 egg
1 teaspoon of vanilla

2 1/2 cups of flour
1 teaspoon of baking soda
1 teaspoon of cream of tartar
1/2 teaspoon of salt
1/2 cup of nuts or chocolate chips

Cream shortening and sugars, then add other ingredients, starting with butter in order given. Roll into balls the size of walnuts. Dip the top half in cold water, then into sugar. Bake on greased cookie sheet for 10-12 minutes at 350°. Makes 3 dozen.

BUTTERMILK COOKIES

1 cup of butter or lard
2 cups of sugar
3 eggs
1 teaspoon of vanilla

3/4 cup of buttermilk
2 teaspoons of baking soda
2 teaspoons of cream of tartar
flour to roll out (about 5 cups)

Cream lard and sugar. Add eggs, beating well. Then add vanilla. Add buttermilk and dry ingredients alternately. Chill dough for several hours. Roll out and cut-out cookies. Sprinkle with sugar and bake at 350° until golden - about 10 minutes for each batch.

CHEWY OATMEAL COOKIES

1 cup of white sugar
1 cup of brown sugar
1 cup of lard
2 eggs
3 cups of oatmeal

2 cups of sifted flour
1/2 teaspoon of salt
1 teaspoon of baking soda
1 teaspoon of vanilla

Cream sugars thoroughly with lard until light and fluffy and no granules remain. Beat in the eggs until light. Stir in oatmeal. In a separate bowl, sift the measured flour with salt, soda, and baking powder. Work into the oatmeal mixture. Mix in vanilla. Drop by teaspoon onto a cookie sheet. Bake at 350° for 10 to 12 minutes.

"Now don't get me wrong, our life isn't all a bed of roses, but I wouldn't live any other way,"

------said by an Amish woman in Hillsdale County, Michigan

KEEPING HOUSE

My husband Ben and I took up housekeeping in the Spring of 1958, which made quite a change in our lives.

A house, garden, and 40 acres of land had to be cared and paid for. Work wasn't so easy to find at that time. Ben looked all over for work, but work (carpenter trade) was slack then. We often think of those first years of starting out on our own. Then in the Spring of 1959, he got in with the Farm Bureau Co-op carpenter crew and has stayed with it ever since. In the summer of 1959, we had our firstborn (a girl).

Then in the fall of 1963, we sold our 40 acre farm and bought the farm we live on now (104 acres). Farm prices then sound very cheap compared to today. Wages, also were lots lower then as Ben worked for $1.40 an hour. But everything is lots higher today, so wages have made a change.

We remodeled our house when we bought it, and put siding on. Years later, though, we tore the south end of our house off and took the siding and old roof off and went with all new material. Building caused a lot of work. Carrying over 1,000 jars from the cellar and putting them in our washhouse and all the other things that had to be moved for the rebuilding, created a lot of labor. Dishes, furniture, everything had to be emptied out before tearing off the south end of the house.

Living was close quarters at such a time. We had to eat out in the washhouse, but in a way, it was enjoyable. We all looked forward to when it was completed. The building went fast and we were soon back in order. We like it very well now, and we have a nicer and bigger cellar.

PIES

NEVER FAIL PIE CRUST

3 cups of flour
1 cup of lard
1 tablespoon of vinegar

1 egg
1/3 cup of water
1 teaspoon of salt

Mix lard, salt, and flour as usual. Add to other ingredients and mix. Makes three pie crusts.

CHOCOLATE PIE CRUST

1 1/4 cups of sifted flour
1/4 cup of cocoa
1/2 cup of shortening
2-3 tablespoons of cold water

1/3 cup of sugar
1/2 teaspoon of salt
1/2 teaspoon of vanilla

Sift flour, salt, and sugar. Mix cocoa in thoroughly. Cut in shortening. Add vanilla. Sprinkle with water. Form into a ball. Roll out. Press into pie pan. Add filling and bake (vanilla pudding is delicious filling in this crust!)

BOB ANDY PIE

2 cups of white sugar
2 cups of milk
1/2 teaspoon crushed cloves
3 eggs (beat yolks and whites separately)

3 heaping tablespoons of flour
1 tablespoon of butter or margarine
1 teaspoon of cinnamon

Mix together sugar, flour, cloves, and cinnamon. Add butter, beaten egg yolks and milk. Then stir in egg whites. Pour into two unbaked pie shells and bake at 350°.

POOR MAN'S BREAD PIE

Crumb bread into an unbaked 9 inch pie shell till it's full. Add 6 teaspoons of sugar, 1 tablespoon of flour, and 2 tablespoons of cinnamon. Fill pie crust with milk. Bake at 350° to 400° until done.

OLD-FASHIONED CREAM PIE

3/4 cup of brown sugar
3/4 cup of white sugar
1/2 cup of flour
1 teaspoon of vanilla
2 cups of cream
pinch of salt
pinch of cinnamon

Mix all ingredients. Pour into unbaked pie shell. Bake in slow oven about 1 hour. Makes 1 pie.

CHOO FLY PIE

1 cup of molasses
1 teaspoon of baking soda
1 cup of sugar
dash of salt

2/3 cup of boiling water
3 1/2 cups of flour
3/4 cup of lard
3 eight inch unbaked pie shells

Mix one cup of molasses, 2/3 cup of boiling water, and 1 teaspoon of soda. Pour mixture into three unbaked pie shells. Then mix 3 1/2 cups of flour, 1 cup of sugar, 3/4 cup of lard, and a dash of salt and put this on top of the mixture that was poured into the pie shells. Bake at 350° until done.

OATMEAL PIE

8 eggs
3 cups of brown sugar
1 pound of margarine

3 cups of light corn syrup
3 cups of rolled oats
2 cups of nut meats

Melt margarine. Cream sugar, margarine, and eggs together. Add corn syrup and rest of ingredients and mix. Pour into four unbaked pie shells. Bake in a slow oven until done.

AMISH APPLE PIE

3/4 cup sugar
1 teaspoon of cinnamon
6-7 cups of sliced apples

1/2 cup of butter or margarine
1/2 cup of brown sugar
1 cup of flour

Mix sugar and cinnamon with apples and put into an unbaked nine inch pie shell. Mix the butter, brown sugar, and flour for topping. Sprinkle over the pie. Bake 15 minutes at 425°, then lower oven temperature to 350° and bake for 30 minutes.

FRENCH RHUBARB PIE

1 beaten egg
1 cup of sugar
1 teaspoon of vanilla
2 cups of rhubarb

2 tablespoons of flour
dash of salt

Mix all of the above ingredients and pour into an unbaked pie shell.

Topping:
3/4 cup of flour
1/3 cup of margarine

1/2 cup of brown sugar

Mix topping ingredients and sprinkle over the rhubarb mixture. Bake pie at 400° for 10 minutes, then at 350° for 30 minutes.

MARY'S CORN MEAL PIE

2 eggs, beaten
1 1/2 cups brown sugar
3 tablespoons of butter or margarine
4 tablespoons of cream
2 tablespoons of corn meal
1/2 cup of nuts (optional)

Mix all the above ingredients together. Pour into an unbaked pie shell.
Bake at 300° for 35-40 minutes.

LEVI'S PECAN PIE

3/4 cups of sugar   2 tablespoons of milk
3/4 cups of corn syrup   2 eggs
1/2 teaspoons of salt   1/2 cup of pecans

Mix and spoon into an unbaked pie shell. Bake at 350° until done.

INDIANA PECAN PIE

1 cup of white corn syrup   3 eggs, slightly beaten
1/2 cup of brown sugar   1 cup of pecans
1/4 cup of melted butter   1 teaspoon of vanilla
1/3 teaspoon of salt

Combine syrup, sugar, salt, margarine, and vanilla. Mix well. Add
eggs. Pour into 9 inch pie shell. Sprinkle pecans over the whole
mixture. Bake in 350° oven for 45 minutes.

LEMON FLUFF PIE

3 egg yolks
1 teaspoon of grated lemon rind
3 egg whites

1/8 teaspoon of salt
1/4 cup of lemon juice
1/2 cup of sugar

Beat egg yolks. Add lemon juice and grated rind. Cook slowly until rather thick. Cool mixture and fold in egg whites, beaten stiff with sugar and salt. Pour into baked pie shell.

SUSAN'S PRIZE-WINNING LEMON PIE

3 tablespoons of cornstarch
1 1/4 cups of sugar
1/4 cup of lemon juice
1 tablespoon of grated lemon rind

3 eggs, separated
1 1/2 cups of boiling water
1- 9" baked pie shell

Combine sugar, cornstarch, lemon juice, and lemon rind. Beat egg yolks; add to cornstarch mixture, gradually adding boiling water. Heat to boiling over direct heat and then boil gently in 4 minutes, stirring constantly. Pour into a pie shell.

Beat egg whites until stiff, but not dry. Gradually beat in 6 tablespoons of sugar. Spread meringue over top of pie. Bake in a hot oven for 4-5 minutes at 425°, or until browned. Cool.

RHUBARB PIE

1 cup of sugar
1 cup of rhubarb

1/2 cup of bread crumbs
2 eggs

Mix. Let stand while. Pour into pie crust, sprinkle with nutmeg and bake.

PENNSYLVANIA DUTCH PEACH CREAM PIE

Filling:
4 cups of sliced, fresh peaches
1 cup of sugar
2 tablespoons of flour
1 egg
1/4 teaspoon of salt
1/2 teaspoon of vanilla
1 cup of sour cream

Crust:
1/2 cup of butter
1 1/2 cups of flour
1/2 teaspoon of salt

Topping:
1/3 cup of sugar
1/3 cup of flour
1/4 cup of butter
1 teaspoon of cinnamon

Crust: Cut butter into flour and salt. Mix. Press into 9 inch pie pan.

Filling: Slice peaches into a bowl. Sprinkle with 1/4 cup of sugar. Let stand while preparing the rest of the filling. Combine 3/4 cup sugar, flour, egg, salt, and vanilla. Fold into sour cream. Stir into peaches.

Pour into crust. Bake at 400° for 15 minutes. Then lower oven temperature to 350°, and bake for another 20 minutes. Then sprinkle the topping evenly over the top of the pie and bake another 10 minutes at 400°.

ELIZABETH'S BEST RHUBARB CUSTARD PIE

3 cups of diced rhubarb
1/4 teaspoon of salt
2 tablespoons of cornstarch
1 tablespoon of butter or margarine

1/2 cup of sugar
3/4 cup of corn syrup
1 egg

Place rhubarb into unbaked crust. Combine sugar, cornstarch, and salt. Add egg and beat well. Add syrup and soft butter. Beat and pour over rhubarb. Bake in 450° oven for 15 minutes then reduce to 350° for 30 minutes or until rhubarb is tender.

CHOCOLATE DREAM PIE

3/4 cup of sugar
1/3 cup of flour
1/4 teaspoon of salt
2 eggs
2 cups of milk

1 tablespoon of butter
1 teaspoon of vanilla
1/2 cup of semi-sweet chocolate chips
1-9 inch baked and cooled pastry shell

In a saucepan, mix sugar, flour, and salt. Add 1 cup of milk, mix until smooth. Bring to a boil over medium heat, stirring briskly. Continue to stir and boil until smoothly thickened. Remove from heat. Beat eggs with remaining 1 cup of milk, gradually stir into hot mixture. Then put back over heat. Bring to a boil, stir until mixture thickens more. Remove from heat. Stir in butter, chocolate chips, and vanilla. Blend until chocolate is melted. Pour into baked pie shell. Chill.

GREEN TOMATO PIE

6 green tomatoes, sliced
1 apple, thinly sliced
1 cup of sugar
3/4 teaspoon of cinnamon

1/4 teaspoon of cloves
1 teaspoon of butter
1 tablespoon of tapioca
1 tablespoon of lemon juice

Arrange half of the fruit in the pie crust. In a separate bowl, mix ingredients, then sprinkle over the fruit in the pie crust. Add the rest of the fruit. Put top of the pie crust on and dot with lemon juice. Makes one pie. Bake at 400° for 35 minutes.

PEANUT BUTTER PIE

2 cups of powdered sugar
1/2 cup of peanut butter
cooked vanilla pudding

Crumb two cups of powdered sugar and 1/2 cup of peanut butter. Take out 1/4 cup of these crumbs. With the rest of the crumbs, divide in 3 baked pie crusts. Then pour vanilla pudding (cooked and cooled) and fill the crusts. Put whipped cream on top and sprinkle with the 1/4 cup of crumbs on top of whipped cream. Serve.

MILLIONAIRE PIE

2 cups of unsifted powdered sugar
1 stick of margarine
1 egg
1/4 teaspoon of salt
1/4 teaspoon of vanilla
1 cup of well-drained, crushed pineapple

2 baked pie shells
1 cup of whipped cream
1/2 cup of pecans

Cream the powdered sugar and margarine, add the egg, salt, and vanilla. Mix well until fluffy. Spread this in 2 baked crusts, chill. Whip cream until stiff. Blend in well-drained pineapple and nuts. Spoon on top of the sugar and margarine mixture. Chill for a couple of hours before serving.

GRAPE PIE

Red or white seedless grapes may be used.

Filling for one pie:

5 1/3 cups of grapes
1 1/3 cups of sugars
1/4 cup of flour
1 1/4 teaspoons of lemon juice
salt to taste
1 1/2 tablespoons of butter

Put grapes in a saucepan without water. Over low heat combine sugar and flour. Mix lightly through grapes. Sprinkle with lemon juice. Dot with butter, put top crust . on. Bake at 425° for 35-40 minutes.

BANANA PIE

2 cups of vanilla ice cream
1 cup of milk
1 package of instant pudding (banana or vanilla)

Beat all ingredients for 1 minute. Pour into baked pie shell lined with sliced bananas. Top with whipped cream, if desired. Ready to serve.

PINEAPPLE SPONGE PIE

2 cups of grated pineapple
2 eggs
2 tablespoons of melted butter
1 cup of sugar

1/3 teaspoon of lemon extract
1 tablespoon of cornstarch

Separate the eggs. Beat the egg yolks, sugar and cornstarch together, add to pineapple with the lemon extract and butter. Cut and fold in beaten egg whites. Pour into unbaked pie shell and bake at 350° for 30 minutes or until done.

CHOCOLATE MOCHA PIE

1 envelope of clear gelatin
1/4 cup of cold water
1 tablespoon of cocoa
3/4 cup of sugar

1/8 teaspoon of salt
1 teaspoon of instant coffee
1 1/4 cups of milk

Soften 1 envelope of gelatin in the cold water. Combine in saucepan with cocoa, sugar, salt, coffee, and milk. Bring to a boil, stir constantly. Take from stove. Stir cooked mixture until smooth. Whip the cream and add to the chocolate mixture. Finally add a teaspoon of vanilla and stir vigorously. Pour into baked pie crust, chill and serve.

STRAWBERRY PIE

1 pie shell, baked
8 ounces of cream cheese
3 tablespoons of cornstarch, mixed with a teaspoon of water

1 cup of sugar
2 pints of strawberries

Soften and stir cream cheese until smooth. Spread evenly over baked pie shell. Slice one pint of strawberries and spread over cream cheese. Crush remaining pint of strawberries and bring to a boil on a range. Add sugar and cornstarch mixture. Then turn down to medium and cook for 2 minutes. Cool and pour over raw strawberries in the pie shell. Refrigerate for several hours before serving.

COCONUT PIE

1/2 cup of brown sugar
1/4 cup of flour
1/2 cup of coconut
1/4 teaspoon of baking soda
1/2 cup of molasses

1/4 cup of sour cream
3/4 cup of milk
1 egg, beaten
19 inch unbaked pie shell

Combine sugar, flour, coconut, and soda. Add molasses, sour cream, milk, and beaten eggs. Mix well. Pour into unbaked pie shell. Bake at 350° for 10 minutes and then at 325° for 35 to 40 minutes.

COCONUT CREAM PIE

2 eggs
1/2 cup of sugar
1/2 cup of margarine
1/2 cup of milk

1 cup of coconut
1/4 cup of flour
unbaked pie shell.

Beat eggs and stir sugar in till lemon colored. Then add rest of ingredients. Mix until smooth. Pour into an unbaked pie shell. Bake 45 to 50 minutes at 350°.

NUT PIE

1 cup of white sugar
1/2 cup of raisins
1 tablespoon of flour
1 tablespoon of vinegar

1/2 cup of walnuts or pecans
2 eggs, beaten
1/2 cup of butter

Mix and pour into unbaked pie shell. Bake at 350° until golden.

RAISIN PIE

No Amish wedding is complete without raisin pie.

Cook one cup of raisins covered with water in a kettle until plump and juicy - about 15-30 minutes on medium. Then in a separate bowl, make a thickening with 2 tablespoons of clear gelatin, a pinch of salt, one cup of sugar, and 1 tablespoon of vinegar mixed with water. Pour into raisin mixture. Cook to your desired thickness. Add some more sugar if it is not sweet enough for you. Pour into an unbaked pie shell. Cover top with dough, seal and flute edges. Cut slit in the center for steam escape. A lattice-top pie crust is often used. Bake at 400° for 30 minutes and serve.

AN EVENING WITH THE COBLENTZES

The evening has arrived and everyone is at home.

The chores completed, the evening meal has been enjoyed together and the dishes are washed. What do we want to do next? Well, it's a cool night and the garden needs some weeding yet. It's getting dark, so we all go in the house. I clean up, take a pen in hand, and write a column with a well-lighted lamp. The girls are reading books and writing letters. My husband enjoys reading in the evenings.

Our evenings are spent in so many different ways. Singing, yodeling, writing, visiting, working, and reading are all ways we pass the time. The evenings are never long enough. With no television or radio, we enjoy our evenings together. Sometimes we have company in the evenings which really speeds up the hours.

Also, we sometimes enjoy playing some games. Last night the caroom board was in use, and the game Aggravation™ is played a lot. Anyway, there seems to be no dull evenings with the family together.

Winter nights are cozy at the Coblentzes, as we usually have our wood-stoves in gear. The stoves provide enough heat to keep everyone safe and warm.

GARDENING

It's a great time of year in the first days of spring to spade for the early garden vegetables. We like to have the garden all plowed in the fall before the snow flies.

The first cool-weather crops are usually planted as soon as the ground is worked. Our first vegetables in the ground consist of onion sets and onions left over from winter. They are called multipliers. Also planted are radishes, lettuces, peas, red beets, carrots, spinach, and some flowers. I enjoy emptying one seed packet after another. Peas do better in cooler weather. Radishes do well by the sign of the moon which we always go by and seem to get good results.

After the first sprouts appear, that means get your hoe in gear, as those tiny weeds will come forth.

When the danger of frost has passed, the more tender vegetables will be planted. I have heard that there is hardly ever a killing frost after the last full moon in May. Plants such as early cabbage, tomatoes, bell and hot peppers, and sweet potatoes can be put in the ground. Also, other vegetables such as sweet corn, green beans, melons, cucumbers, and zucchini can be planted. Later on, we plant winter radishes, and late and Chinese cabbage. Sweet corn is planted at various times, so we can have sweet corn all summer. Meal-planning is so much easier when you have a garden.

Look what a garden can do. Plenty of salads can be prepared and lots of jars can be filled and canned for the coming winter. Since we have no electricity to freeze our corn and peas we have to can for our winter supply. It is always good to see those jars fill up from our hard, but enjoyable, work in the garden!

CAKES

QUICK CARAMEL FROSTING FOR CAKES

4 tablespoons of brown sugar
2 tablespoons of butter

4 tablespoons of milk
powdered sugar

Mix in a saucepan and let come to a boil on the stove. Then let cool and thicken with powdered sugar to desired consistency. Makes enough to spread onto one cake.

RHUBARB CAKE

1 1/2 cups of brown sugar
1/2 cup of shortening
1 egg
1 1/2 cups of fresh rhubarb
1/2 teaspoon of salt

2 cups of flour
1 cup of buttermilk
1/2 teaspoon of baking soda

Combine shortening, sugar, and egg. Beat till light and fluffy. Combine soda, salt, and flour together. Add to shortening mixture. Alternately with buttermilk, fold in the rhubarb. Mix well. Pour into greased 9X13 pan and bake at 350° for 30-40 minutes. Top with whipped cream if desired.

SALAD DRESSING CHOCOLATE CAKE

1 1/2 cups of sugar
2 cups of flour
pinch of salt
3 tablespoons of cocoa

2 teaspoons of baking soda
1 cup of warm water
1 cup of salad dressing
1 teaspoon of vanilla

Mix ingredients for 2 minutes. Bake 30 minutes at 350° in 2 greased layer-cake pans.

ARLENE'S FAVORITE CHEESECAKE

1 package of lemon Jello
1 cup of boiling water
8 ounces of cream cheese
1/2 cup of sugar
1 teaspoon of vanilla
1 can of whipping cream
2 cups of graham cracker crumbs
1/2 cup of butter
1/2 cup of sugar

Mix graham cracker crumbs, butter, and sugar and set aside. Dissolve Jello in boiling water. Chill until slightly thickened. Cream together cheese, sugar, and vanilla. Add Jello and blend well. Fold in stiffly whipped cream.

Pack 2/3 of the graham mixture on the bottom and sides of a 9X13X2 inch pan. Add filling and sprinkle with remaining crumbs.

EICHER CAKE

1/2 cup of shortening
1 3/4 cups of brown sugar
3 eggs, separated
1 cup of sour cream
1 teaspoon of baking soda

2 teaspoons of cinnamon
1 teaspoon of crushed cloves
1 teaspoon of allspice
2 cups of flour
1/2 teaspoon of salt

Mix sugar and shortening. Add egg yolks. Mix in flour, soda, and spices. Add sour cream and beat well. Add vanilla and fold in stiffly beaten egg whites. Bake in a greased 8 inch layer pan for 30 minutes at 350°.

BIRTHDAYS

Many people around here have surprise birthday parties when their children turn the age of 21, if they still are at home and unmarried.

They usually try to have a surprise on them before their birthday arrives. The person to be surprised is usually taken somewhere and on their return, the young people of the community are at the house waiting to surprise the unsuspecting, soon-to-be 21-year-old.

Most places, cakes, candy bars, snacks such as potato chips, pretzels, crackers, and pop are served at the parties. Some also serve ice cream.

In the evening, the one who turned 21 opens his or her many gifts. Also lots of singing and yodeling takes place.

Following is a birthday cake recipe:

RED DEVIL'S FOOD CAKE

2 cups of sifted cake flour
1/2 cup of shortening
1 1/2 cups of sugar
1/3 cup of cocoa
2 eggs

1/2 cup of milk
2 teaspoons of baking soda in milk
1 cup of boiling water
1 teaspoon of vanilla

Cream the shortening and then add sugar, cocoa, eggs, and beat well. Add flour and, after that, the baking soda. Add boiling water and vanilla. Rub butter or lard into a cake pan and pour in the batter. Bake for 30 minutes at 350°.

AMISH ANGEL FOOD CAKE

1 1/4 cups of sifted cake flour
1 teaspoon of vanilla
1 3/4 cups of sifted white flour
1/4 teaspoon of salt
1 1/2 cups of egg whites (about 10-11 eggs)
1 1/2 teaspoons of cream of tartar

Sift together flour and 3/4 cup of sugar twice. In a large mixing bowl, beat egg whites, cream of tartar, salt and vanilla until foamy. Beat in remaining 1 cup of sugar - 2 tablespoons at a time. Stir vigorously until meringue holds stiff peaks that are glossy and moist. Divide flour and sugar mixture in 4 parts. With rubber spatula, gently fold each portion into meringue until flour and sugar mixture disappear. Push batter into ungreased 10 inch tube pan. Gently cut through batter once with a spatula to remove air bubbles. Do not lift it out of the batter while doing this.

Bake in moderate oven (375°) for 35-40 minutes or until cake springs back when lightly touched with finger. Invert pan and let cake cool before moving.

PEACH UPSIDE-DOWN CAKE

1 quart of sliced peaches
1 cup of white sugar
6 tablespoons of margarine
2/3 cup of shortening
1 teaspoon of salt
1 cup of white sugar
1 cup of brown sugar
2 eggs
2/3 cup of shortening
2 teaspoons of vanilla
2 cups of flour
2 1/2 teaspoons of baking powder

Drain peaches, reserve syrup. Melt butter in a skillet; add brown sugar, 2 tablespoons syrup and drained peaches. Add water to remaining syrup to make 1 cup; set aside. Cream together shortening and sugar until light; add eggs and vanilla. Beat until fluffy. Sift together the dry ingredients; add alternately with the 1 cup of syrup. Spread over peaches. Bake in 350° oven for 40-45 minutes. Other fruit may be used in place of peaches.

CHOCOLATE ANGEL FOOD CAKE

2 cups of egg whites
1 1/2 cups of sugar
1/4 teaspoon of salt
1/4 cup of cocoa
1 teaspoon of cream of tartar

1 teaspoon of vanilla
3/4 cup of cake flour

Sift flour, cocoa and salt together. Add cream of tartar to egg whites and beat until stiff peaks. Add vanilla, then sugar gradually and fold in flour mixture. Put in ungreased tube pan and bake 40-45 minutes at 350°-375°.

PINEAPPLE UPSIDE-DOWN CAKE

1/4 cup of softened butter
1/4 cup of brown sugar
1/2 cup of corn syrup
2 cans of crushed pineapple, well-drained

1 box of yellow cake mix
nuts, if desired

Follow the directions for the yellow cake as usual. In a separate bowl, mix butter, sugar, corn syrup, and pineapple and put into greased pan. Then mix cake and put on top. Bake at 350° for one hour. Serve upside-down with whipped cream.

CHOCOLATE CHIP CAKE

1 3/4 cups of sifted flour
1 teaspoon of baking soda
1 cup of shortening
1 teaspoon of vanilla
2 eggs, beaten

2 tablespoons of cocoa
1 teaspoon of salt
1 cup of boiling water
1 cup of sugar
6 ounces of chocolate chips

Sift together flour, cocoa, salt, and baking soda. Cream shortening and sugar. Add eggs and vanilla. Beat thoroughly. Add water and flour alternately, mixing batter until smooth after each addition. Spoon and spread into a greased 13X9 inch pan. Sprinkle top with chips. Bake at 350° for 45 minutes.

BUTTERMILK CAKE

2 cups of sugar
1/2 cup of butter
2 cups of buttermilk
3 1/2 cups or more of flour

2 teaspoons of baking soda
1 teaspoon of cinnamon
1/2 teaspoon of nutmeg
1/4 teaspoon of allspice

Mix well and pour into a cake pan. Bake at 350° until golden. Delicious!

BUTTERSCOTCH CAKE

1/2 cup of butter
1 cup of packed brown sugar
3 eggs
1 teaspoon of vanilla
2 cups sifted all-purpose flour

1 teaspoon of baking soda
1 1/2 cups of buttermilk
1 cup of quick oats
6 ounces of butterscotch chips

Mix together butter and sugar. Blend in eggs and vanilla. Stir well. Sift together flour, salt, and soda. Add to butter mixture alternately with milk, mixing after each addition. Stir in oats. Pour into greased 9X13X2 inch baking pan. Sprinkle butterscotch chips onto the batter. Bake at 350° for about a half hour. Let cool before cutting.

VANILLA CAKE

1 box of yellow cake mix
1 stick of butter
2 eggs
1 box of powdered sugar
2 eggs

1-8 ounce package of cream cheese
1 teaspoon of vanilla
1 cup of chocolate chips

Mix cake mix, melted butter, and eggs and pour into a baking dish. Mix powdered sugar, cream cheese, eggs, and vanilla together. Add chips. Pour this mixture on top of cake batter. Do not mix. Bake for about 45 minutes at 325°.

BREAKFAST

CHAPTER 5

For the Coblentz family, the day begins before the dark has lifted from the surrounding fields. At 4 a.m., an hour when most Americans are sound asleep, Elizabeth begins breakfast for her husband and daughters. Morning chores are completed, such as milking the cows, feeding livestock, and bringing in firewood.

A hearty, but simple breakfast is served. The Coblentzes often eat scrambled eggs and fried potatoes for their morning meal. Freshly-brewed coffee perks on a wood stove, filling the house with the steaming aroma of dawn.

Elizabeth's 88-year-old mother enjoys a coffee soup for her breakfast. Elizabeth's daughters, who are a little more contemporary, enjoy oatmeal cookies with their morning meal.

BACON AND EGG BAKE

6 slices of bacon
1/2 medium onion
salt and pepper
1 can of cream of mushroom soup

5 hard boiled eggs, diced
2 cups of shredded cheese
1/4 cup of milk

Heat oven to 350°. Fry bacon until crisp. Remove from skillet, drain fat, reserving 2 tablespoons. Fry onions in the tablespoons of fat. Stir in soup, milk, cheese, eggs, and seasonings. Pour into baking dish, top with crumbled bacon. Bake 20 minutes. Serve over biscuits. Feeds 5.

LA GRANGE COUNTY GRIDDLE CAKES

2 cups of buckwheat flour
2 eggs, beaten
2 teaspoons of sugar
2 teaspoons of baking powder

1/8 teaspoon of salt
1 1/2 cups of milk
1/2 cup of water

Mix in a bowl until smooth. Bake on a hot griddle till golden.

MORNING MOLASSES MELT CEREAL

1 cup of rolled oats
1 cup of corn meal
3 cups of whole wheat flour
1/2 cup of sugar
2 teaspoons of baking powder

1 teaspoon of baking soda
2 teaspoons of salt
3/4 cup of molasses
1 1/2 cups of milk

Mix the dry ingredients together. In a separate saucepan, heat the milk and add molasses. Mix with dry ingredients. Bake in shallow pan in moderate oven (about 350°). Cool and slice into strips. When dry, grind well. Serve with milk or eat plain as a snack.

FARM FRENCH TOAST

Beat 2 eggs, add 3/4 cup of milk. Dip pieces of bread in the mixture. Melt and lightly brown butter in a pan. Put in the bread pieces and sprinkle with salt. Fry until brown on both sides. Serve with hot syrup, fresh berries, or preserves.

EGG-IN-NEST

1 tablespoon of butter
1 slice of bread

1 egg
salt and pepper to taste

Put one tablespoon of butter into a small, hot skillet. Butter the bottom of pan. In the butter, place the slice of bread. We cut a hole in the bread with a water glass. Drop the egg in the hole. Then we toast the cut-out bread in the skillet.

CHEESY SCRAMBLED EGGS

Break 4 eggs into a bowl. Add 1/4 to 1/2 cup of diced cheese. Add salt and pepper. Pour into a hot, greased frying pan. Stir vigorously with a fork, breaking the yolks. Fry and serve quickly.

SCRAMBLED EGGS AND BACON

1/4 pound of bacon
8 eggs
1 cup of milk

3/4 teaspoon of salt
1/8 cup of butter, melted

Fry bacon; drain and crumble. Put eggs in a bowl. Beat lightly. Add milk, salt, and butter. Add crumbled bacon last. Grease pan. Bake in 12X9 inch pan at 425° till knife comes out clean. Serves 10 to 12 people.

CREAMED EGGS

6 eggs
6 tablespoons of butter
6 tablespoons of flour

1 1/2 teaspoons of salt
3 cups of milk
dash of pepper

Hard boil eggs. Peel and set aside. Melt butter in heavy saucepan. Add flour and seasoning. Stir until well-blended. Slowly add milk, stirring constantly. Cook until smooth. Chop eggs and add to sauce. Serve on hot toast. Feeds 6 to 8 people.

CORN MEAL CAKES

3 cups of sweet milk
3 eggs, beaten
1 teaspoon of salt
1 tablespoon of sugar
1 teaspoon of vanilla

2 tablespoons of melted butter
1 pint of corn meal
1 pint of all-purpose flour
1 teaspoon of baking soda
a couple of pinches of baking powder

Stir well. Beat eggs and then add milk and vanilla, then dry ingredients. Bake on a hot griddle until golden. Serve with preserves or syrup.

SUSAN'S SUNRISE SAUSAGE SUPREME

1 pound of lean sausage
6 eggs, whipped
3/4 teaspoon of dried mustard

2 1/2 cups of milk
2 cups of grated cheese
8 slices of bread

Cube the bread and place on the bottom of a 8X13 inch pan. Brown sausage and drain. Spread over the bread. Whip eggs in a bowl and add the dry mustard and milk. Sprinkle the cheese on top. Refrigerate overnight. Next morning, mix 1 can of mushroom soup and 1/2 can of milk. Pour over top of casserole and bake at 350° for 45 minutes. Serves 8 to 10 people.

QUICKIE OMELET

4 eggs
1/8 teaspoon of pepper
1 tablespoon of softened butter

1/4 teaspoon of salt
1 tablespoon of flour
1 tablespoon of water

Beat egg whites with salt until stiff, but still moist. Beat together other ingredients till fluffy. Then fold in egg whites. Pour in well-greased skillet (hot enough to sizzle water). Cover tightly, cook low for 8 to 10 minutes - until surface is dry when touched. Fold. (Mushrooms, ham, cheese, or bacon can be added before folding). Serves 1 or 2.

CORN MUSH

Bring three cups of water to a boil. In a bowl, make a thickening with one cup of cornmeal, one teaspoon of salt, and 1 cup of water. Add this mix to the boiling water. Stir mixture until it has reached the boiling point, then stir occasionally. Cook for 15-20 minutes, then pour into a deep baking dish. Cool, then slice and fry until brown. My mother used to eat it frequently. She liked to eat it with milk.

ELIZABETH'S OWN SCRAMBLED EGGS

I take 6 eggs and crack them into a bowl, and put in some sausage, a couple of slices of cheese, a few diced-up hot peppers, and mix it all together with salt and pepper. I put it in a skillet to fry with margarine or lard until done.

Variation: any kind of meat can be used. Bacon chopped in goes good.

HIDDEN EGGS

4 tablespoons of butter   6-7 eggs
5-6 slices of bread
Cheese, any amount, any kind

Melt butter in a foil pie pan. Save half of the melted butter for the top. Break up enough bread to cover the bottom of the pie pan. Drop eggs on the bread and season with salt and pepper. Break another piece of bread on top and drizzle with melted butter. Dot with cheese. Bake at 350° for 15 to 20 minutes or until the eggs are done.

LOVINA'S BREAKFAST PIZZA

1 package of pizza crust mix (or make your own crust)
1 pound of bulk sausage
1 cup of hash browned potatoes
1 cup of shredded cheddar cheese
4 eggs
3 tablespoons of milk
1/2 teaspoon of salt
pepper to taste
2 tablespoons of grated Parmesan cheese

Preheat oven at 375°. Brown sausage and drain. Cool. Prepare crust as directed on package. Spoon cooled sausage over the crust. Sprinkle with potatoes and Cheddar cheese. Beat eggs, milk, salt and pepper together. Pour over potatoes and cheese. Sprinkle with the Parmesan cheese. Bake 30 minutes at 375°. Slice and serve.

BEFORE SUNRISE OMELET

10 slices of buttered bread
1 pound of chopped ham (bacon or grated cheese or a combination of the three)
6 eggs
3 cups of milk

Lay 10 slices of buttered bread on the bottom of a 9X13 baking dish. Cover the bread with the ham. In a separate bowl, mix the eggs and milk. Pour over the bread and ham. Let set overnight in a cool place (in your refrigerator). In the morning, bake for one hour at 350°. Serves over 6 people.

EGG DUTCH

5 eggs
pepper to taste
1 cup of milk

1 teaspoon of salt
1 heaping tablespoon of flour

Put into a bowl in the order given and beat. Pour into a heated, greased skillet and cover with a tight lid. Place over medium low heat. Cut and turn when half done and finish baking. I usually put cheese on top when almost done. Bacon bits can also be added.

SAUSAGE AND EGG DELIGHT

3 eggs, beaten
1 cup of milk
1 slice of crumbled bread
1/2 teaspoon of salt

1/2 teaspoon of mustard
1/2 pound of sausage or bacon
1/2 cup of grated cheese

Brown your choice of meat in pan and drain off grease. Beat eggs in a large bowl, add milk, salt, and mustard. Then add bread and mix well. Add cheese and meat last. Pour into a small baking dish. Bake 45 minutes at 350°.

BREAKFAST CASSEROLE

8 slices of bread, cubed
1 pound of sausage, fried and drained
6 eggs
2 cups of milk
1/4 cup of margarine
1/2 teaspoon of dried mustard
1 pound of grated cheese
1/2 teaspoon of salt

Put bread in the bottom of a casserole dish. In a separate bowl, beat eggs and add milk, onion, salt, and mustard. Sprinkle sausage and cheese over the bread. Slice margarine over the cheese, and pour the egg mixture over all. Bake 45 minutes to one hour at 325°.

HASHED BROWN POTATOES

1 1/2 pounds of potatoes
1/8 teaspoon of pepper
2 tablespoons of salad oil or bacon drippings
2 tablespoons of finely chopped onion

1/2 teaspoon of salt
2 tablespoons of butter

Cook pared potatoes. Cool slightly. Shred enough potatoes to measure 4 cups. Toss potatoes with onions, salt, and pepper. Heat butter and oil in 9 or 10 inch skillet. Pack potato mixture firmly in skillet, leaving 1/2" space around the edge. Cook over low heat 10 to 15 minutes or until bottom crust is brown. Cut potato mixture in fourths. Turn each portion. Add 1 tablespoon of salad oil if necessary. Cook until brown.

HAM BREAKFAST CASSEROLE

12 slices of day-old bread
a half a dozen slices of thick ham
6 slices of Cheddar cheese

Salt and pepper to taste
6 large eggs
3 cups of milk

Separate mix: 1 cup of crushed corn flakes and 1/4 cup of melted butter

Butter 9X12 inch dish. Lay 6 slices of bread in dish. Top with ham and cheese. Lay remaining 6 slices of bread on top, making a sandwich. Beat eggs and mix with milk. Pour over sandwiches. Dash salt and pepper over the mixture. Sprinkle corn flakes and butter mixture over all of it. Chill overnight. In morning, bake for an hour at 325°.

CEREAL

1 1/2 cups of brown sugar
8 cups of oatmeal
4 cups of whole wheat flour
2 teaspoons of salt
2 packages of crushed graham crackers
1 pound of chocolate chips
1 pound of butterscotch chips

2 1/2 cups of melted butter
3 teaspoons of baking soda

Stir all together (except for chocolate and butterscotch). Bake in slow oven for 45 minutes. When finished add 1 pound chocolate chips and 1 pound of butterscotch chips immediately. Stir vigorously and serve.

READER FLASHBACK

Elizabeth's first column, August, 1991

The Amish Cook weekly newspaper column debuted in "The Quincy (Ill.) Herald-Whig" in August of 1991. As of this printing, the column appeared in over 30 newspapers.

This has been a rushy morn, but enjoyable. We still have five girls here at home yet. Four went to work as usual. They all leave by 6:00 to 6:30 a.m. The girls were all busy doing my cleaning before they left. Working all together like this is what I call real family life. With no boys at home, the girls go out to help do the milking and other chores around the barn. We have one daughter and two sons married and I feel lucky to have five grandsons and five granddaughters. Guess we just don't appreciate all our good health enough.

The kitchen has the smell of freshly baked pies. There is a tour planning to stop in this afternoon (all senior citizens), so we like to serve them some pie and a drink to the 40 or 50 people. It is so good to go in the garden to get rhubarb and get apples from our trees to bake some pies. The pies I baked this morn are: 3 apple, 1 rhubarb, 4 lemon, 2 oatmeal, and 2 blueberry. I will share the recipes of the oatmeal and apple pie with you readers. I know you'll like it once you give it a try. Looks like my youngest daughter has work for us again. She just picked 1 1/2 bushels of green beans. So we must can them. Good luck!

Editor's Note: *Briefly, a couple of years ago, Elizabeth opened her home to a few tourists at the request of the local chamber of commerce. She has since discontinued doing this.*

READER FLASHBACK

APPLE BUTTER AFTERNOON, October, 1991

This column depicts the traditions that revolve around seasons. Apple harvesting time in the fall, hog-butchering in the winter, gardening in the spring, and canning in the summer are some of the many such seasonal activities that Elizabeth writes about in her columns. These events are typical of most Amish families.

The fall harvest has been completed in the fields, so the rush has come to a halt.

It reminds me of apple butter cooking at my brother's place. Their family and our family got together, usually in late October, to prepare for the apple butter cooking in a copper kettle. My brother, Christian, made a stand outside for the kettle. We always hoped for a nice day to cook it but we got caught with rain at times. The evening before, we peel and *snitz* (Pennsylvania Dutch for "cut") the apples, usually about 30 gallons or more. Some additional cider was bought also. It depends on how many gallons we wanted when cooked. The next morning, the 40-50 gallons of cider was to be cooked down in the copper kettle to a certain amount.

My brother always had certain marks on a yard stick as to how far the cider was to be cooked down, when the apples are put in, and when the sugar is added. After the sugar was added, it didn't take long to take the copper kettle from the fire. Then we carried the apple butter by the three gallon stainless steel buckets. The apple butter was then put into jars to seal.

The house usually had the aroma of freshly cooked apple butter. It is so delicious with home-baked bread. Must say, my brother had the hardest job of all, as he looked after everything.

READER FLASHBACK

LATE WINTER 1992

As Elizabeth's mother ages, the children rally around her, alternating care between them. This is a late winter writing that gives a peek in the Coblentz home.

We've had a couple of days of sunshine now. I hope Old Man Winter has gone to rest. We need the sunshine. Some people are putting out gardens and taking care of berry patches.

My husband went back to work again after being a shut-in for quite sometime with pneumonia. I guess with this changeable weather, he just couldn't hack it. He is still under the doctor's care.

Mother was 87-years-old Sunday. Our family all visited her home for the Sunday evening meal plus my husband's brother and wife and son. While washing supper dishes, we decided to sing "Happy Birthday" for her. We all walked over to my sister's place, a few houses away from us. Mother is staying with my sister for the present time. She greatly appreciated all of us coming.

Well, we just took a quilt out of frame, with this being dinnertime now. Tomorrow, a week ago, I put a quilt in frame, marked off what you call diamond. The girls and I sewed on it in the evenings or whenever we had a chance of being idle. With the five girls and I, it was like having our own quilting bee in the evenings (the girls are working during the day). It is enjoyable in the evenings, with singing and yodeling, as the girls quilted. Even my husband got in on it to keep the needles threaded for us. Ha!

I have two more quilts marked off to be put in frame and, hopefully, to do them right away. Those are marked off with a four leaf clover pattern. I guess our fingers need a rest until next week. See you readers later!

READER FLASHBACK

The following is a selection written by Elizabeth during the Spring of 1993. This letter walks the reader through a typical day with Elizabeth, or any Amish mother and wife, for that matter.

4 a.m. Time to get up to start the day. I made a breakfast of fried potatoes, eggs, and bacon. I also fixed toast, which gets done sometimes in the oven of our range. Breakfast is being prepared on our range. Naturally, I always put water over in the stainless steel tea kettle for coffee. Ben and one of our daughters went out to the barn to get the chores done.

4:50 a.m. Everyone is seated at the table for breakfast.

5:10 a.m. The girls are all helping wash breakfast dishes and getting the house in order for the day.

5:30 a.m. Two of the girls left for work at the sewing factory. The older one has been working there for nine years, the other one for two years.

6:15 a.m. Ben usually leaves for work (carpenter trade), but he's going to be home today. They were going to put up a building, but the man wasn't quite ready to start it today.

7:30 a.m. Done with the laundry. It is drying so nice out there on the clothesline. Beautiful day! Ben is getting the garden ground ready so we can plant the garden. What a relief!

8:30 a.m. Son Albert and his little son, Ben, are here now. He's wanting to help haul the manure. They're getting the manure-spreader and the team of horses ready to haul.

8:45 a.m. One of our daughters went to clean a house in town for a nice lady, although I could use her help now, since the weather is nice to put out a garden.

10 a.m. My youngest daughter and the writer are putting the garden out. She's 17 today. Brings back memories, as it was a Monday when she was born at 6:30 p.m.

11 a.m. Went in to get dinner, as I've got menfolk working hard, hauling loads and loads of manure with the manure-spreader which is driven by our team of horses.

Noon Dinner!

1 p.m. Looks like rain. Susan and I hurry out to the garden to get more vegetable and flower seeds planted.

2 p.m. We had a downpour which chased us out of the garden, but the menfolk kept unloading manure.

3 p.m. Back in the garden - it didn't rain that much.

4 p.m. Menfolk finished up their job of hauling manure. The girls are home from work. Albert is leaving for home soon. Little Ben is probably tired by now. He was a busy little body today. Was enjoyable to have him around.

4:30 p.m. Girls are getting supper. They're barbecuing chicken and our sugar-cured ham out on the grill. We want a special meal in honor of Susan's 17th birthday.

5 p.m. Done for the day in the garden.

6 p.m. Suppertime! A couple of families came for supper in honor of Susan's birthday. So the rest of the evening will be spent celebrating that, and then it will be time for bed.

GROCERY SHOPPING

Since we are living in times when the dollar doesn't seem to go very far when buying groceries in the store, you watch for bargains. Coupons also help a lot.

Bread, potatoes, flour, meats, sugar, and yeast are items you usually have to have. If I don't bake bread every week, I have to buy it in the store. We buy our potatoes as we hardly ever grow them in the garden. Meats are often bought in the stores. We like chicken or steak to be grilled and summer sausage for the lunch buckets. We used to make our own summer sausage, but since the boys are married we just don't make any. It always is so handy to have around to snack on on a busy day, for lunch or to serve when someone comes to visit. This is the recipe, we always used.

CANADIAN SUMMER SAUSAGE

66 pounds of ground beef
33 pounds of pork
4 tablespoons of salt

5 pounds of white sugar
1/3 pound of pepper
2 ounces of saltpeter

Mix as you would for sausage and stuff tightly in muslin sacks (3 1/2 to 4 inches wide and 2 feet long). Hang in a cellar for 1-2 weeks and then smoke. Let dry for 6-8 weeks. Good eating!

GRANDMA'S GATHERINGS

New Year's Day was always a great day to look forward to going to Grandpa and Grandma Schwartz's. They had 14 living children and over 100 grandchildren, plus great grandchildren. Everyone always tried to be present on New Year's Day. Happy memories!

Some of the families would go early in the morning to sing the New Year's song to Grandpa. They would arrive for breakfast. How tired Grandma must have been to start the day off like that.

A good noon meal was served to all. The big table was reset quite a lot of times.

Lots of singing and yodeling took place when they all got together.

In the afternoon, Grandma and Grandpa would hand out gifts to their children and the grandchildren, each got a sack of candy and some kind of dish or hanky. I have saved those, and they now carry many memories

On December 17, 1944, Grandpa Chris J. Schwartz died, and what a sad New Year's that was, to be together without our Grandpa. But Grandma always had the New Year's gathering afterwards. She died on October 31, 1956. So that ended the gatherings at Grandpa's.

GRANDMA'S - Continued

Then my folks, Amos Grabers, started having their family gatherings on New Year's Day, which we all looked forward to, but then father died and there were no family gatherings during the holiday season.

Now, we have our married children and have our own Christmas gatherings. At present, our family count is 32. They all gather here, at Ben and Elizabeth Coblentz's for breakfast, dinner, and the whole day. We have set up a long table so we can all be seated at one time.

Frying eggs for 32 people is somewhat different, but enjoyable. We also have fried potatoes, bacon, ham, cheese, toast, home-baked bread, orange juice, coffee, and all those other goodies of the holidays.

Lots of singing and yodeling gets done in the afternoon. We have all kinds of snacks, candy, and cheese balls. Who would be hungry for an evening meal? Gifts are also exchanged during the day. Such an enjoyable day to be together again!

COURTSHIP AND DATING

Sunday evening arrives and the young folks look forward to all being together for singing and sometmes a meal at someone's house. After visiting for a bit, they enjoy playing volleyball and some have a ball game out in the field. When it gets later, they gather in the house or in a well-cleaned shed with tables and benches set up and they sing out of our church songbook, called the *Ausbund.* After singing quite a few songs, they yodel and sing other songs and the evening passes on for all to leave for their homes around 10:30 to 11 p.m. They're usually sixteen years old or older when they join the young folks for singing.

If a boy is interested in going steady with a young girl, he will ask to take her home. And this will begin a weekly pattern of "seeing each other" at Sunday evening singings. As the courtship progresses, they will begin to exchange letters and cards through the mail, and see each other through the week, sometimes for dinner with the family. Sometimes the courtship process can last for many years. Most Amish men and women marry by their mid-20s.

The Amish retain over 70 percent of their church members.

MAIN DISHES

CHAPTER 6

BUSY MOTHER'S CASSEROLE

2 cans of mushroom soup
2 cups of milk
2 cups of cheese
Salt and pepper to taste
Any amount of meat you choose (dried beef, ham, or hamburger)

2 cups of uncooked macaroni
4 boiled eggs, diced
1/2 cup of onion, diced

Heat mushroom soup, and gradually add milk. Mix in remaining ingredients. Put in 4-quart casserole. Place in refrigerator overnight; bake uncovered in 350° oven for 1 hour.

SUNDAY SUPPER

2-12 ounce cans of tuna
2 cans of cream of chicken soup
1 cup of regular rice
3 cups of potato chips
2 cans of cream of mushroom soup

4 cups of celery
1 cup of chopped onions

Combine all ingredients in a bowl, except for the chips. Pour into a greased glass baking dish or casserole. Crush potato chips and sprinkle over the top. Bake 1 1/2 hours at 350°.

COUNTRY CHICKEN CASSEROLE

1-10 1/2 ounce can of chicken
2 cups of noodles
1 pint of milk
1/2 pound of cut cheese, any kind

2 cans of mushroom soup
1 onion, chopped fine

Mix all above ingredients well. Pour into a casserole dish and refrigerate overnight. The next day, bake for one hour at 350°.

CHICKEN LOAF

One 5 pound chicken, cooked and cubed
2 cups of uncooked rice
2 cups of bread cubes
salt and pepper to taste

2 cups of chicken broth
2 cups of milk
4 eggs
2 cups of diced celery

Stir and mix all ingredients. Spoon into a greased baking dish. Bake at 350° for 1 hour or until a knife comes out clean when inserted in the center of the loaf. Serve in slices. Feeds quite a few people (about 20).

AMISH MEAT LOAF

1 1/2 pounds of ground beef
3/4 cup of rolled uncooked oats
1/4 cup of chopped onion
3/4 cup of milk

1 1/2 teaspoons of salt
1/4 teaspoon of pepper
1 egg, beaten

Combine all ingredients and mix thoroughly. Pack firmly into a loaf pan.

Sauce:
1/3 cup of catsup
2 tablespoons of brown sugar

1 tablespoon of prepared mustard

Combine the sauce ingredients and pour over meat loaf. Bake in preheated 350° oven for one hour. Let stand five minutes before slicing.

PLAIN MEATLOAF

1/2 pound of ground beef
2 beaten eggs
1/4 cup of chopped onion
1/4 teaspoon of pepper

2 teaspoon of salt
1 cup of tomato juice
3/4 cup of uncooked rolled oats

Combine all ingredients thoroughly and pack firmly into a pan. Bake at 350° for one hour. Let set for a few minutes, slice and serve.

ONE-DISH MEAL

2 cups of sliced potatoes
1 cup of canned beef

3/4 cup of noodles
3/4 cup of tomatoes

Cook potatoes, beef, and noodles about 1/2 hour. Add tomatoes and cook for 10 minutes. Salt to taste.

HAY STACK SUPPER

crushed saltine crackers
plenty of cooked hamburger
lettuce
cooked spaghetti

Cheese sauce: Melt some American or cheddar cheese over low heat and gradually add milk to make a sauce.

Layer on top of each other in the order given in a large bowl. Pour cheese sauce over top, and serve.

CHEESE BAKE

4 slices of bread
2 tablespoons of butter
1 teaspoon of prepared mustard
2 eggs
1 teaspoon of salt

1/4 teaspoon paprika
1 1/2 cups of milk
1/2 pound of colby cheese
4 slices of bacon

Blend butter and mustard. Spread onto the bread slices and place in a casserole dish. Beat eggs, salt, and milk. Pour onto bread. Cut bacon in 2 inch pieces and lay on top. Sprinkle with paprika. Bake 30 minutes in a 350° oven and serve at once.

MOTHER'S MEALS

The Amish have always been known for their thrift and ability to make elegant meals out of the most basic ingredients. The Great Depression influenced the Amish just like the rest of American society. Farms were hit hard by drought and supplies were often short.

"Mother would often make real simple meals for us, a lot different than the food we eat today," says Elizabeth. Following is a sampler of those basic meals:

BROWN FLOUR SOUP

Take 2 tablespoons of flour and brown in lard in a skillet, adding 1 cup of water to it when browned. Then add 1 cup of milk. Season with salt and pepper to your taste. Bring to a boil and pour this over cubed bread (about two or three slices) in a bowl

COLD MILK SOUP

Sweeten milk with sugar and pour over crumbled bread and strawberries in a bowl. Mulberries and bananas also made for a good cold soup. We could change the soup as different fruits came in and out of season.
Elizabeth's mother is now 88-years-old and still enjoys these meals.

HAMBURGER CASSEROLE

2 pounds of hamburger
1/2 teaspoon of black pepper
1/2 teaspoon of salt
16 ounce can of tomato sauce
1 cup of cooked rice

1/4 cup of chopped onion
3/4 cup of chopped green pepper
1 tablespoon of chili powder
2 cups of shredded cheese

Cook hamburger and drain excess grease. Mix cooked hamburger and the rest of the ingredients together in a large casserole dish, save one cup of cheese to spread on top. Bake at 350° for 20 minutes.

WASHDAY CASSEROLE

3 pounds of hamburger
9 slices of bacon
3 onions
3 cups of potatoes
3 cups of celery

2 cans of cream of mushroom soup
3 cups of cooked spaghetti
1 quart of tomato juice
1 pound of Cheddar cheese

Brown hamburger and onions in a pan. Pour into casserole and add potatoes, celery, and spaghetti. Pour mushroom soup over top. Fry bacon and lay on top. Pour tomato juice over this. Add cheese over that. Bake for 1 1/2 hours in a 350° oven.

ECONOMY STEW

2 potatoes, sliced
1/2 cup of celery, chopped
1 can of tomato soup
1 pound of lean, uncooked hamburger

1 cup of onion, chopped
1 can of pork and beans
salt and pepper

Put potatoes, onions, and celery on the bottom of a casserole dish. Dash it with salt and pepper to taste. Put beans on top of the bottom layer, then tomato soup, and cover with uncooked hamburger. Bake for 2 hours at 350°.

AMISH CASSEROLE

2 pounds of hamburger
1 package of noodles

2 cans of cream of mushroom soup
2 cans of tomato soup

Brown hamburger and drain. Cook noodles and drain. Mix all ingredients in a casserole dish and bake at 375° for 1/2 hour.

YAMAZETTI

1 package of noodles
1/2 pound of Cheddar cheese
1 1/2 pounds of ground beef
1 chopped onion

1 can of evaporated milk
1 can of tomato soup
1 green pepper, chopped
Salt and pepper to taste

Cook noodles for about 10 minutes and then drain. Brown the meat and onion, adding salt and pepper to taste. Place ingredients in a baking dish as follows: 1 layer of noodles, 1 layer of meat, 1 layer of cheese, 1 layer of green peppers. Repeat. Then add evaporated milk and soup. Bake for 1 hour at 375°.

NOODLE CASSEROLE

1 pound of hamburger
1 pound of noodles
a pinch of cheese

2-10 ounce cans of cream of chicken soup
tomato juice to taste

Brown hamburger, season to taste. Cook noodles, then mix in the soup and a little tomato juice (1/4 - 1/2 cup). Mix hamburger and noodle mixture in a casserole dish. Top with your favorite cheese. Place in the oven at 350° just long enough to melt the cheese.

CHICKEN NOODLE CASSEROLE

1 chicken - 2 or 3 pounds	10 ounces of noodles
1/2 cup chopped green pepper	1 can of mushrooms
salt and pepper to taste	1 1/2 cups of cheese

Cook chicken and remove from bones. Cook noodles in broth until soupy. Add chicken, peppers, mushrooms, and cut-up cheese. Top with buttered bread crumbs. Bake at 350° for 1 1/2 hours.

CHICKEN AND DUMPLINGS

1 whole chicken	1 teaspoon of salt
1 small onion	3 medium potatoes, diced
1 teaspoon of parsley	1 pint of peas
1/4 teaspoon of sage	

Boil chicken until tender. Pick from the bones. Add other ingredients and bring to a boil. Prepare dumplings as follows:

Dumplings: 1 1/2 cups of flour, 1/2 teaspoon of salt, 2 teaspoons of baking powder, 1 egg, 1/3 cup of melted oleo, 3 tablespoons of milk.

Mix all dry ingredients and then add egg and milk and stir just until moistened. Drop dough from teaspoon into boiling broth. Cover tightly for 15 minutes. Do not uncover until ready to serve.

BAKED CHICKEN

Cut-up a chicken. Melt 1/2 cup of margarine and mix in a cup of lightly crushed Rice Krispies cereal. Roll chicken pieces in the Rice Krispie mixture. Sprinkle salt and pepper on it. Bake in an oven at 350° for one hour or until done. We also sprinkle seasoning salt on the chicken which makes for a better taste.

TUNA DELIGHT

8 ounces of noodles
3 1/2 tablespoons of butter
3 tablespoons of flour
2 to 2 1/2 cups of milk

1/2 cup of grated cheese
salt
pepper
7 ounces of tuna

Cook noodles until soft and done. Drain and put in a casserole dish. Then stir in other ingredients. Sprinkle the top with cheese. Bake at 350° for an hour.

SIMPLE TUNA CASSEROLE

2 cans of tuna
1/2 cup of milk
1 can of mushroom soup

crushed potato chips

Blend tuna, soup, and milk in a casserole dish. Cover with crushed chips. Bake uncovered for an hour at 350°.

HUM-A-TUNA

1/2 cup of sliced celery
2 tablespoons of chopped onion
1 tablespoon of butter

1/2 cup of milk
1-7 ounce can of tuna
2 tablespoons chopped pimento

In a saucepan, cook celery and onion in butter until tender. Blend in soup, then slowly stir in milk. Add tuna and pimento. Heat, stir. Serve over rice, top with parsley. Makes 4 servings.

TUNA SURPRISE CASSEROLE

8 ounces of packaged noodles
3 tablespoons of butter
3 tablespoons of flour
2 to 2 1/2 cups of milk
1 cup of chopped ham

1/2 cup of grated cheese
salt
pepper
7 ounce can of tuna

Cook noodles until tender. Drain and put into baking dish. Add tuna and ham and mix slightly. Use remainder of ingredients to make a white sauce. In a small saucepan, melt butter, then mix in flour. Add milk, cheese, and seasonings. Stir until sauce thickens. Pour over noodle-tuna mix. Bake in 350° oven for 30 to 40 minutes

INDIANA AMISH DRESSING

1 whole loaf of bread
3 eggs, well-beaten
2 tablespoons of butter
3 cups of chicken broth

4 tablespoons of chopped celery
1 medium onion
1/2 teaspoon of poultry seasoning
salt and pepper to taste

Toast bread, cut in cubes. Combine celery, onion, and seasonings. Bring broth to boil and add to bread and celery. Add eggs last. Bake 1 hour at 350°.

PLAIN MEATBALLS

4 pounds of hamburger
1 cup of diced celery
1 medium onion
4 eggs
3 teaspoons of salt

1 teaspoon of pepper
1 can of mushroom soup
1 can of milk
oleo or bacon grease

Mix the above ingredients (except for the milk and soup) very well. Shape into balls. Brown in oleo or bacon grease. Arrange in a roaster.

Sauce: 1 can of mushroom soup, 1 soup can full of heated milk. Stir together and pour over meatballs. Cover the dish and heat at 350°.

ONE-KETTLE SUPPER

1 quart of beef
1 quart of home-made noodles
4 potatoes, diced

salt and pepper to taste
1 medium onion

Cook potatoes, noodles, and onion together in a big pot or kettle on top of the stove until done. Add beef. Cook until hot. Beef soup base can be used in place of beef. This is a very good meal on a busy day.

LASAGNA

8-10 ounces of wide noodles
16 ounces of tomato sauce
Large package of cream cheese
1/2 cup of sour cream
1/4 cup of chopped green pepper

2 pounds of hamburger
8 ounces of tomato paste
1 1/2 cup of cottage cheese
1/2 cup of chopped onion

Cook noodles. Drain. Add small amount of olive oil to noodles while cooking. Combine cheeses, sour cream, onion, and peppers. Brown meat and drain off grease. Add tomato sauces. Alternate noodles, cheeses, tomato sauces, and meats in a baking dish. Repeat layers once. Bake at 400° for 45 minutes.

SWISS BEEF

Slice a chunk of beef very thin. Season it with salt and pepper, stacking the slices on top of each other. Put lard in a small frying skillet about half full when melted, and make it real hot. Then stir seasoned slice of beef with a fork a couple of times on one side and then on the other side. Put in a bowl, and it is ready to eat.

SHIPWRECK

1 pound of hamburger
1 medium onion
5 medium potatoes

1 can of cream of mushroom soup
1 soup can full of milk

Brown hamburger and put in baking dish. Dice in a layer of onion and then layer potatoes on top of the onion. Pour soup on top and cover with a soup can full of milk. Bake at 350° for 90 minutes.

GERMAN RAVIOLI

3 cups of flour
5 eggs
3 tablespoons of oil
1/2 pound of hamburger
2 teaspoons of salt
2 slices of bread, soaked in water
chopped parsley

1/2 cup of water
1 teaspoon of salt
1 onion
1/2 pound of sausage
1/2 teaspoon of pepper
2 tablespoons of grated cheese

Blend flour, water, 3 eggs, and salt. Knead lightly. Place back in bowl, cover, let set for 15 minutes. Roll dough out and cut into small squares. Brown meat and onion in oil. Combine with remaining ingredients and place some in center of dough squares. Place another square on top and seal the edges with fork or fingers. Cook ravioli in boiling water for about 10 minutes. Drain. Serve with a tomato-based sauce.

BEN'S FAVORITE POTATO CASSEROLE

2 pounds of sliced potatoes
1/2 cup melted butter
1 teaspoon of salt
1/2 cup of chopped onion

1 can cream of chicken soup
2 cups of grated cheese
2 cups of sour cream
1 package of crushed crackers

Mix all of the above ingredients well, except for the cracker crumbs, and place in a 2 quart casserole. Sprinkle cracker crumbs on top. Bake in 350° oven for 45 minutes.

LANCASTER COUNTY CASSEROLE

2 tablespoons of butter, melted
2 pounds of onions, cut in 1/4 slices
3/4 pound of thinly sliced ham
4 or 5 baking potatoes, peeled and sliced
2 tablespoons of flour
salt
fresh, chopped green pepper
2 cups of tomato juice
2 cups of corn

Lightly grease a 3-quart casserole dish with some of the butter. Layer the onions on the bottom, then ham, and then potatoes. Sprinkle flour over the mix and season with salt and pepper. Pour tomato juice and corn over and then add boiling water to completely cover potatoes. Dribble remaining butter on top and bake uncovered 3 hours. Stir hourly. Ready to serve after 3 hours.

CHEESE-BAKED POTATOES

These should be frozen for one week before eating!

7 baking potatoes   salt and pepper
2 teaspoons of chopped onion   paprika
2 tablespoons of butter   shredded cheese

Bake potatoes in a 425° oven for 1 hour. Cool. Cut into halves. Scrape the potato from shells into a bowl and mash. Add a little milk to make it fluffy. Brown onions in butter. Stir in potato mixture along with salt and pepper. Pile mixture into 12 shells. Cover tops with shredded cheese. Sprinkle on paprika. Place shells in flat freezing container. Seal. Freeze for one week. Place frozen potato shells on baking sheet. Bake at 450° for 25 minutes.

POTATO PATTIES

1 1/4 cups of flour
1/4 teaspoon of salt
1 egg

1 cup of milk
3-4 potatoes, sliced

Dry potatoes on paper towels. Mix flour and salt in a bowl. Add egg and milk and beat until smooth. Dip slices into batter one at a time and drop into hot fat. Fry until gold brown.

HOMEMADE PIZZA DOUGH

2 cups of flour
2 teaspoons of baking powder
1/2 teaspoon of salt

2/3 cup of milk
6 tablespoons of salad oil

Measure flour, baking powder, salt, milk, and salad oil into a bowl. Stir vigorously until mixture leaves the side of the bowl. Gather dough together and press into a ball. Knead dough in bowl 10 times to make smooth. Place on a pizza pan or baking sheet. Turn up edge 1/2 inch and pinch or pleat. Add favorite toppings and bake at 425° for 30 minutes.

HOMEMADE PIZZA SAUCE

3 gallons of tomato juice

3 or 4 chopped onions

Cook these until tender and sieve. Add:

1 cup of sugar
1/2 cup salt
1 tablespoon of paprika
1 tablespoon of chili powder

1 tablespoon of red pepper
2 tablespoons of garlic salt
2 teaspoons of oregano

Add all of this to the cooked juice, thicken slightly with clear gelatin. Stir and boil well. Cold pack for 10 minutes.

132

MOTHER'S PIZZA SAUCE

10 cups of tomato juice   4 large bay leaves
1 large onion

Soak, separate, and strain. Add the following:

1/2 cup of salad oil   1/4 teaspoon of red pepper
4 tablespoons of salt   2 teaspoons of oregano
4 teaspoons of sugar   1 1/2 teaspoons of garlic powder
1/2 teaspoon of pepper

Bring to a boil and add 3/4 cup of clear gelatin and boil again. Makes 5 pints.

PIZZA PIE

1 package of dry yeast   3 cups of flour
1 cup of warm water   1 teaspoon of sugar
1 1/2 teaspoons of salt   1/4 cup of salad oil

Topping:

2 cups of tomato sauce   1 pound of your favorite cheese

Dissolve yeast in warm water. Add sugar, salt, and oil and mix thoroughly. Add 1/2 of the flour and beat until there are no lumps. Gradually add remaining flour. Knead dough for 5 minutes. Take half of the dough, roll out to a circle 12 inches in diameter. Place on a greased cookie sheet. Leave edges a little thicker than the middle. Repeat this with the other half of the dough. Put on a second cookie sheet, let rise 20 to 30 minutes. Brush the tops with salad oil. Cut one pound of cheese in fine pieces and sprinkle over top. Put 2 cups of tomato sauce lightly over the cheese. Bake at 450° for 15 minutes or until edges are brown and the cheese is melted.

QUICK PIZZA

4 English muffins
1/2 cup of chili sauce or pizza sauce
1/2 to 1 teaspoon of salt
1/4 teaspoon of pepper

1/2 teaspoon of oregano
1/2 pound of sausage
3/4 cup of grated cheese

Split muffins into halves. Toast cut side and spread with pizza sauce. Mix salt, pepper, and oregano. Sprinkle over sauce. Cut each sausage in fourths, place over muffins. Top with cheese. Sprinkle with Parmesan cheese. Broil till hot through and cheese is melted.

AMISH QUICK PIZZA

1 pound of ground beef
1 cup of shredded cheese
1 can of pizza sauce

1/2 teaspoon of oregano
Parmesan cheese
hamburger buns

Heat meat until brown and then drain. Quickly blend in cheese, pizza sauce, and oregano. Spread mixture on buns and sprinkle with cheese. Heat at 425° for 3 or 4 minutes.

VEGETABLE PIZZA

2 tubes of crescent rolls
3/4 cup of mayonnaise
1/2 cup of sour cream

1 large package of cream cheese
1 package of Ranch dressing mix
Finely grated Cheddar cheese

Assorted vegetables: chopped green peppers, sliced tomatoes, sliced onion, and mushrooms.

Spread crescent rolls out on baking sheet for the crust. Bake for 7-10 minutes. Mix all of the above ingredients (except vegetables and Cheddar cheese) together until creamy and spread over the crust. Put vegetables on top of this mixture. Cover with plastic and chill for 3-4 hours. Serve cold.

PIZZA CASSEROLE

1 pound of hamburger (drained, browned with onions)
1/2 bag of dumpling noodles (cooked and drained)
2 jars of pizza sauce
1/2 pound of shredded cheese

Cover bottom of 9X13 inch baking dish with 1 jar of pizza sauce and add noodles. Sprinkle hamburger over noodles. Add some more pizza sauce. Top with cheese. Bake at 325° for 45 minutes covered.

SEVEN LAYERS CASSEROLE

1 cup of uncooked rice
1 can of tomato sauce
1/2 a tomato sauce can of water
1/2 cup of chopped onion
1/2 cup of chopped pepper
1 pound of uncooked ground beef
1 can of tomato sauce
1/4 a tomato sauce can of water
4 strips of bacon
1-16 ounce can of corn

In a 2 quart casserole layer the ingredients as given at the left. Rice first, then corn, etc. Be sure to blend the water and tomato sauce together before pouring into the dish. Cover and bake for 1 hour at 375°. Uncover and bake for another 1/2 hour at 325°-350°.

SKILLET CASSEROLE

One pound of hamburger, prepared fresh.
fresh grated potatoes
1 onion
1 can of cream of mushroom soup
1/2 dozen or more slices of cheese

Spread the hamburger on the bottom of a large skillet. Put the potatoes on top of the hamburger, then dice the onion on top of the potatoes. Pour the soup on top of that, and then top it off by layering slices of cheese over the whole layered casserole. Cover skillet and simmer for 40 minutes. Very good casserole! Carrots can also be added.

LUNCH BUCKETS

It seems easier to pack lunch buckets now-a-days than it did 50 years-ago or more. We have store bought items today to put into lunch buckets. Years ago, we made simple things to put into them.

We were glad when a bologna sandwich was in our lunch pail instead of apple butter or mustard sandwiches. Now the children prefer a better kind of meat for a sandwich.

Now when packing lunch buckets you think of nutrition as the key, and not too many sweets or rich foods.

BOLOGNA AND CHEESE SPREAD SANDWICHES

1 small onion
3 slices of cubed bologna
1 thick slice of longhorn cheese, shredded
2 sweet pickles, diced
3 or 4 small, crushed crackers
Enough of your favorite dressing to make a spread

Mix the above ingredients until you get a creamy spread. Put between bread, and you've got a good sandwich!

LUNCH BUCKETS - Continued

Here is another good recipe for the lunch pail:

HAM SALAD SANDWICHES

2 cups of ground, cooked ham   1 large dill pickle
3 stalks of celery
11/4 teaspoons of dry mustard
1/4 teaspoon of onion powder
1/2 cup of mayonnaise
1/2 teaspoon of salt
1 tablespoon of lemon juice

Put ham, celery, and pickle through a coarse food chopper blade. Add remaining ingredients. Mix well and spread onto sandwich bread.

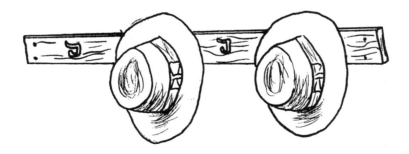

FOOD PRESERVATION

Having leftover food at one time was hard to keep, with no icebox. When Ben and I got married and bought a farm that had no basement, Ben cut a 50 gallon wooden barrel in half and put it in the ground. He made a lid for it, and that is where the leftover food went. It felt quite cool in the barrel. But I knew meat wouldn't keep too long in there.

When I was a little girl at home, mother used to have a bucket of cold water to keep the milk jars in - which helped it not to sour by evening. Although, on hot muggy days, it would sour before evening. Every once in awhile, we would have to change the water during the day to keep the milk in the jar cold.

Today, big ice chests and iceboxes are in use. Some also use old deep freezers. We fill the deep freezers with blocks of ice that we buy from the store. Basements are also used to keep foods cool - I am glad our basement seems cool. (**Editor's Note:** *The deep freezers that Elizabeth makes reference to here, are the large free-standing floor kind that can be bought at any major department store. Of course, there is no place to plug them in, so they use giant ice blocks. The floor freezers hold the cold in very well*).

Ben will arrive home with a large, 2 foot long, block of ice. Using ice tongs, he places the block in the icebox. This does a lot to keep foods cool.

For cans and jars of fruits, vegetables, soups, and meats, the basement is used for cool storage. It seems to work well. Foods that need to be frozen, such as some fresh meats, are kept on the blocks of ice.

A group of Pennsylvania Dutch people, called German Baptists, are allowed to have electric refrigerators in their homes. Some Mennonites are also permitted to own them.

SPAGHETTI CASSEROLE

1 pound of spaghetti
1 pound of ground beef
28 ounce can of tomatoes

1/2 pound of Provolone cheese
1 can of cream of mushroom soup

Cook spaghetti in salt water until tender. Drain. Brown ground beef and drain excess fat. Combine spaghetti, ground beef, tomatoes, cheese, and soup in a casserole dish. Bake at 350° for 30 minutes.

POOR MAN'S STEAK

1 1/2 pounds of hamburger
1/2 cup of cracker crumbs
1/2 cup of milk or water

salt and pepper to taste
1 onion, if desired
1 can of cream of mushroom soup

Mix all of the above ingredients very well and press into a baking dish so the layer is 1 inch thick. Chill overnight. In the morning, cut in squares, roll in flour, and fry in butter. Put in casserole dish and smother with 1 can of cream of mushroom soup. Bake for 1 1/2 hours in a slow oven (about 300°).

BARBECUE BURGERS

2 slightly beaten eggs
2 teaspoons of salt
1/4 cup of minced onion

2 cups of soft bread crumbs
2 pounds of hamburger
1/4 cup of milk

Combine above ingredients and mix well. Shape into thin patties. Broil over hot coals, brushing both sides with barbecue sauce (see following recipe).

BARBECUE SAUCE:

2 tablespoons of brown sugar
2 tablespoons of vinegar
2 tablespoons of Worcestershire sauce

1 cup of catsup

Stir and brush over meats.

BUSY DAY DINNER

In a large iron skillet, melt 1 tablespoon of butter. Line the bottom of the pan with a thick layer of onions. Cover the onions with potatoes. Sift two tablespoons of flour over the potatoes. Pour a small bottle of tomato juice over the potatoes. Slice some sausage or ham and thinly cover the potatoes and tomato juice. Cover the whole mixture with boiling water. Salt. Bake slowly for the afternoon (about 3 hours). Very good, and economical dinner!

GOOEY BOLOGNA SANDWICHES

1/2 pound of ground bologna   3/8 pound of American cheese
1 tablespoon of pickle, chopped   1/3 cup of mayonnaise
2 tablespoons of onion, chopped   1 or 2 tablespoons of mustard

Mix all ingredients very well. Spread on a wiener bun and wrap in foil. Bake 15-20 minutes at 350°.

DELICIOUS HAM

1 cup of bread crumbs   dash of pepper
1 cup of milk   three whole cloves
1 diced onion   1/4 cup of brown sugar
1/2 teaspoon of salt   1 cup of water
a large 2 inch raw ham steak

Stir all the ingredients except for the ham in a mixing bowl. Place the ham in a baking dish and pour the mixture over the ham. Bake in a 400° oven for three hours.

BARBECUED SPARERIBS

2 tablespoons of butter
1 cup of garlic
3/4 cup of water
1 teaspoon of dry mustard
1/4 teaspoon of pepper
2 tablespoons of lemon juice
1 teaspoon of salt
2 tablespoons of Worcestershire sauce

1 sliced onion
1/2 cup of celery
1 cup of catsup
2 tablespoons of vinegar
2 tablespoons of brown sugar

Soften and then melt butter. Mix in onion and cook until nice and brown. Add the rest of the ingredients and cook 20 minutes. Makes 2 1/4 cups of liquid. Pour over ribs in a roaster. Bake ribs until done. The last hour, baste frequently with the sauce. Bake at 375°.

MENNONITE CASSEROLE

1 1/2 pound ground beef
onion, browned
1/2 pound of drained noodles

salt
pepper
1 can of peas

Cheese sauce: 1 quart of milk and 8 tablespoons of flour, and strips American cheese. Melt ingredients in a saucepan, for a thick sauce, use more cheese, for a thinner sauce, use less.

Pour cheese sauce into a casserole dish and mix in ground beef, noodles, seasonings, and peas. Bake for 1 hour at 450°.

TRUST ME CASSEROLE

1 1/2 pounds of hamburger
salt and pepper to taste
2 cans of cream of chicken soup
1 can of cream of celery soup

4 cups of milk
1 loaf of bread

Fry the hamburger. Add soups and milk. Make it thick by adding bread crumbs. Pour mixture into a casserole dish and bake at 350° for one hour.

141

PIZZA CASSEROLE

8 ounces of noodles, cooked
1 pound of hamburger
1 cup of diced onion
1 cup of diced cheese (your favorite)

1 cup of sour cream
1 cup of pizza sauce
1 cup of cottage cheese

Cook noodles, then add onion, sour cream, and cottage cheese. Put in baking dish by layers. Season to your taste. Bake at 350° for about an hour.

SALMON PATTIES

1-1 pound can of salmon
1 egg
1 tablespoon of flour
3/4 cup of cracker crumbs

1 teaspoon of chopped onion
1 tablespoon of lemon juice
3/4 cup of milk

Mix. Shape into patties. Brown both sides of patties in a skillet before serving.

DELICIOUS PORK CHOPS

5 pork chops
1 cup of bread crumbs
dash of pepper
salt to taste

1 egg, beaten
1/4 cup of milk
1/4 cup of boiling water
3 tablespoons of fat

Add seasonings to bread crumbs. Beat egg and stir in milk. Dip chops in liquid and coat in crumbs. Brown chops in fat in skillet. Place chops in a baking dish and add boiling water, enough to cover the bottom of the pan. Cover pan and bake at 400° for a little less than an hour.

CHURCH CASSEROLE

2 pounds of boiled potatoes, peeled and chopped
4 tablespoons of melted butter
1 teaspoon of salt
1 can of undiluted cream of chicken soup
1 pint of sour cream
2 cups of sharp cheese
2 cups of crushed corn flakes, mixed with 1/4 cup of butter
1/2 cup of chopped onion
1/4 teaspoon of pepper

Combine potatoes and butter in a large mixing bowl. Add salt, pepper, onion, soup, sour cream, and cheese. Mix thoroughly. Spoon into a greased casserole dish (9X13). Cover with crushed corn flakes and butter. Bake at 350° for 50 minutes.

SNOOZER SANDWICHES

1 cup of catsup
1/2 cup of water
1/2 teaspoon of mustard
2 tablespoons of vinegar

1 1/2 pounds of ground or sliced ham
1/3 cup of brown sugar

Stir in a casserole dish and bake at 250° for one hour. Spoon onto bread and serve as a sandwich. Very good!

WIGGLERS

2 pounds of hamburger
5 slices of bacon
1 1/2 cups of celery
1 can of mushroom soup
1 package of spaghetti

2 onions, diced
2 cups of cooked potatoes
1 quart of tomato soup

Fry bacon. Take out of skillet and fry hamburger and onios in the bacon grease. Put in the bottom of a roaster and put the cooked potatoes, carrots, celery, peas, and mushroom soup on top. Then pour the cooked spaghetti, bacon, and tomatoes on top. Bake for 1 hour at 350°.

143

HOBO SUPPER

6 weiners, sliced
6 medium potatoes, precooked and diced
2 tablespoons of onions, cut-fine
1/4 cup of butter
1 pint of peas
1 can of cream of mushroom soup

1 pint of corn

Stir into a casserole dish. Bake at 350° for 30 minutes.

SPAGHETTI PIE

6 ounces of cooked spaghetti, drained
2 eggs, well-beaten
1/3 cup of Parmeasan cheese
2 tablespoons of butter
1 any-sized jar of homemade or store-bought spaghetti sauce
1-2 cups of cottage cheese

Mix all together. Put some spaghetti sauce in bottom of a casserole. Pour spaghetti on top of sauce. Spread 1-2 cups cottage cheese on top of spaghetti. Pour rest of sauce on. Bake 20 minutes at 350°.

DINNER SAUSAGE

1 pound of pork sausage
1 onion, chopped
1 can of cream of mushroom soup

1/2 cup of milk
1 cup of diced cheese
1 small package of noodles

Fry crumbled sausage long enough to fry out fat, but don't cook until crisp. Drain. Brown onion. Cook noodles and drain. Mix all ingredients together in a casserole dish and bake at 325° for a half hour.

CORN-HUSKING BEE

Who knows what a corn-husking bee is?

Well, we used to go to these bees years ago. There are still some people around here that have them, but they aren't as common.

Menfolk take the team of horses and wagon to the corn field when the harvest is ready to be husked. They jerk the ears of corn with the husk on and haul it back to the barn or a shed. This makes a long pile of corn ready to be husked. In the evening, the young people are invited to help husk the corn by lantern light. Benches are set-up in front of the corn, so the job can be done sitting down. The husk is sorted. The clean white husk goes into a box and is put into a place to be kept clean. Then the white husk is taken into the house to be put in a big sack (size of a bed) with four openings in it. They stuff the husks inside till the sack is full. This is then used as a mattress.

There's lots of singing and yodeling going on all evening. After this is completed, everyone goes in the house for soup, sandwiches, or something to drink. There are still corn-husking bees today, but most people use regular store bought mattresses now - although a few still have the husk-filled ones. Lots easier and less dust with a store-bought mattress, I'd say.

My children have never been to a corn-husking bee, so all I can do is explain how it was when I used to go to them - it was lots of fun.

SWISS NOODLES

3 cups of flour
1 teaspoon of salt
1/4 teaspoon of nutmeg

4 eggs, beaten
1/2 cup of water
1/4 cup of butter

Sift flour, salt, and nutmeg together in a bowl. Pour eggs and 1/4 cup of water into the middle of the flour mixture. Beat with a wooden spoon. Add enough water to make the dough slightly sticky, yet keeping it elastic and stiff. Using a colander with medium holes, press the noodles into a large pot full of boiling water. Cook noodles in the water about 5 minutes or until they float to the surface. Lift noodles out and drain on paper towels. Brown noodles in butter over low heat.

CHICKEN POT PIE

1 chicken, cooked and cubed
1 can of cream of chicken soup
3 cups of chicken broth

1 pint of peas
1 pint of cooked carrots
salt and pepper to taste

Combine above ingredients and pour into 9X12 pan. Then follow these instructions for the crust:

CRUST:

1 1/2 cups of flour
1 tablespoon of baking powder
3/4 teaspoons of salt

1 1/2 cups of milk
6 tablespoons of melted butter

Mix well and pour over chicken mixture. Do not stir after you have poured the crust. Bake at 400° for 30 minutes or until crust is golden.

SWEET AND SOUR SAUCE FOR MEATS

8 ounces of cream cheese
1/2 cup of dairy sour cream
1/4 cup of milk

2 tablespoons of sugar
1 tablespoon of vinegar
dash of salt

Combine ingredients, mixing until blended. Serve over cold ham sandwiches.

VEGETABLES

CHAPTER 7

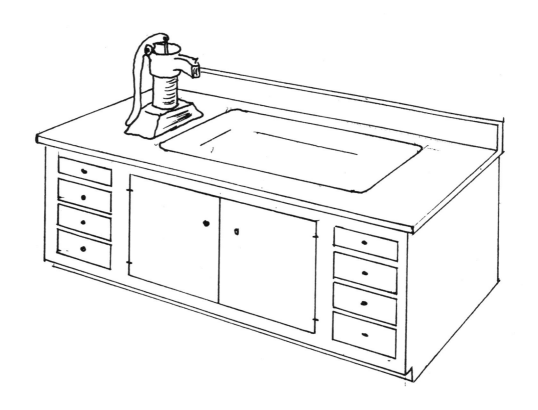

PENNSYLVANIA CABBAGE ROLLS

2 pounds of cabbage
2 pounds of pork sausage
one large onion, chopped
4 pounds of sauerkraut

1 teaspoon of garlic salt
1 cup of raw rice
2 slices of milk-soaked bread
2 cans of tomato soup

Mix above and wrap in cabbage leaves. Blanch 2 heads of cabbage in hot water. Put a layer of cabbage leaves in the bottom of a baking dish. Alternate cabbage rolls and layer of sauerkraut. Add about 3 cans of tomato soup over the top. Bake in 300° oven for 4 hours.

BAKED SWEET CORN

1 quart of sweet corn
1 tablespoon of flour
sugar and salt to taste
celery leaves

2 beaten eggs
1/2 cup of sweet cream
1 cup of crumbled crackers

Mix all together. Grease pan, bake at 350° for 30 minutes or until done.

ELIZABETH'S BACON BEANS

1 1/2 pounds of fresh, cleaned green beans
1/2 small onion
8 slices of thick, cut bacon
1 teaspoon of salt

Simmer all ingredients together in water until beans are tender and fully cooked.

CREAMED POTATOES

Cook four diced potatoes and make a milk thickening with two tablespoons of flour. When potatoes are about done, add the milk and flour thickening and cheese of any amount (Usually 1/2 to 1 1/2 cups grated).

LEAH'S BAKED POTATOES

6 medium potatoes   1/2 cup of cracker crumbs
4 tablespoons of melted butter

Pare potatoes, wash and drain. Cut into thirds, lengthwise. Dip in melted butter and roll in crumbs. Place in greased pan and sprinkle with salt. Bake at 350° for 35-40 minutes.

ZUCCHINI PATTIES

2 cups of grated and drained zucchini   1 teaspoon of pepper
1 egg   1 teaspoon of salt
6 tablespoons of flour   1 small onion, chopped fine

Mix the above ingredients well. Shape into patties and fry until golden.

ZUCCHINI CASSEROLE

1 pound of hamburger
4 cups of zucchini
2 or 3 tomatoes, chunked
onions
American cheese
buttered bread crumbs

Brown hamburger and put into a casserole. Cover with sliced zucchini. Peel tomatoes, cut into chunks to cover zucchini. Dice onion and sprinkle over tomatoes. Add a layer of cheese over tomatoes, top with buttered bread crumbs. Bake 45 minutes at 350°.

INDIANA ZUCCHINI CASSEROLE

1 medium zucchini   4 slices of bread
1 large onion   1 grated pepper
1 tomato   2 tablespoons of butter
sliced cheese   salt and pepper

Cube bread and melt butter. Mix the bread and butter. Layer all of the above ingredients in a casserole dish twice. Put cheese on last. Bake at 350° for one hour.

MARINATED CARROTS

4 cups of sliced, cooked carrots
1 cup of sugar
1/2 cup of salad oil
3/4 cup of vinegar
1 teaspoon of prepared mustard

1 teaspoon of salt
1 teaspoon of pepper
1 medium onion, thinly sliced
1 green pepper, chopped
1 can of tomato soup

Mix carrots, onion, and peppers lightly. Mix the rest of the ingredients in a separate bowl. After it is mixed well, combine with the carrot mixture. Refrigerate at least 12 hours before serving.

BATTER-BAKED PEPPERS

1/2 cup of cut-up jalapeno
1 cup of cut-up sweet peppers
3/4 cup of cut-up onions
1 1/4 cups of flour
1/4 cup of cornmeal
1 tablespoon of baking powder

1 teaspoon of salt
2 eggs
1 cup of milk
2 tablespoons of vegetable oil

Mix the first three ingredients and set aside. Then blend the rest of the ingredients very well. This is your batter. Stir vegetables into the batter. In an iron skillet put 2 extra tablespoons of oil and pour the batter-vegetable mixture in. Bake at 375° for 45 minutes or until very well browned.

FRENCH FRIED ONION RINGS

3 large onions
1/2 cup of milk
1 egg

3/4 cup of flour
1/2 teaspoon of salt

Mix batter. Dip in onion rings and fry in oil until brown.

HOT PEPPERS

The hot pepper seeds are usually put in pots, although I start mine out on the open land. We used to not hear or didn't really know anything about eating these hot peppers, but somehow our family got "addicted" to them. The first time we had some was when we were to Ben's cousin's and they served them with a good meal. This was a couple of years ago.

We canned a lot of hot peppers last year, as they did so well in our garden. Rainy weather must've been good for them.

We dice them in scrambled eggs for breakfast, and also put them on our pizzas. In so many ways you can dice them in some kind of food.

Our married children and even some of our small grandchildren enjoy seeing those peppers on the menu, when coming for a meal.

Our family also eats them for breakfast with fried potatoes, eggs, ham or bacon, toast, and cheese. Try them, you'll like them!

Editor's note: The gradual introduction of hot peppers into Amish society is one of the most significant culinary events in Pennsylvania Dutch culture in this century. Even their swtich to prepared grocery store foods didn't affect the flavor of Amish cooking as much as did the influx of new spices finding their way into the kitchens of Amish cooks.

ONION PATTIES

3/4 cup of flour	2 teaspoons of baking powder
1 tablespoon of sugar	1 teaspoon of salt
1 tablespoon of cornmeal	3/4 cup of milk
2 1/2 cups of finely chopped onions	

Mix flour, sugar, cornmeal, baking powder, and salt. Mix very well. Then add your milk. Stir vigorously to make a nice, heavy batter. Add onions to the batter and stir vigorously. Drop by spoonful into a deep skillet of fat. Turnover in the skillet until each side is golden. Flatten them after you turn them

SIMPLE SWEET POTATO CASSEROLE

6 sweet potatoes
1 cup of brown sugar
1/4 cup of butter

Boil the sweet potatoes until they are partly cooked. Then peel and cut in half. Melt butter in a 9 inch casserole dish. Put in layer of potatoes and sprinkle with brown sugar. Dot with butter and a little salt. Repeat layers until filled. Bake 15-20 minutes at 400°. Marshmallows may be layered on top and browned before serving.

FRENCH FRIED CAULIFLOWER

1 medium-sized cauliflower	3/4 cup of flour
2 egg yolks	1/2 cup of milk
salt to taste	

Wash cauliflower in salted water, then drain. In a separate bowl, beat the egg yolks until light. Salt. Add flour. Beat until smooth. This is your batter. Dip each section of cauliflower into the batter. Fry in a skillet until golden.

CHEESE SAUCE FOR VEGETABLES

2 tablespoons of flour
1/2 pound of any flavor hard cheese, cubed
2 tablespoons of butter
1/2 teaspoon of salt
1 1/2 cups of milk

Melt butter in a saucepan. Add flour and salt and stir. Then add milk slowly. Add cheese and heat until cheese melts and sauce bubbles. Pour over vegetables, toast, potatoes, or macaroni.

BUTTER-BAKED BEANS

1/2 cup of cut-up jalapenos
1 cup of cut sweet corn
3/4 cup of cut-up onions

Mix these three ingredients and set them aside.

Then stir together:

1 1/4 cups of flour
1/4 cup of cornmeal
1 tablespoon of baking powder
1 teaspoon of salt

2 eggs
1 cup of milk
2 tablespoons of oil

Blend these ingredients together to form a batter. Then stir in the set-aside vegetables. Put in an iron skillet with two tablespoons of hot oil. Brown lightly. Then place them in a baking dish and bake at 350° for 45 minutes.

QUICKIE VEGETABLE DISH

1-16 ounce can of lima beans
1-12 ounce can of whole kernel corn
1- 16 ounce can of tomatoes
5 tablespoons of butter
1/2 teaspoon of onion salt
1/2 teaspoon of celery salt

In a one and a half quart casserole, combine all of these ingredients except the butter. Dot the top with butter. Bake in a 350° oven for 1/2 hour or more.

BROCCOLI SOUFFLÉ

8 ounces of cottage cheese
3 eggs
1 package of frozen, chopped broccoli, cooked and drained
3 tablespoons of flour
4 tablespoons of butter
4 ounces of American cheese
salt and pepper
onion to taste

Place cottage cheese in a mixing bowl. Add eggs and stir, then add broccoli. Sprinkle flour on top and mix well. Add butter and stir in some of the cheese. Season with salt, pepper, and onion to taste. Sprinkle remaining cheese on top. Bake one hour in a buttered 1 quart casserole.

STUFFED BAKED POTATOES

8 medium potatoes
5 tablespoons of oleo
salt and pepper

1/2 cup of milk
1 cup of grated cheese

Cut off tops of potatoes after they have baked in oven for about an hour at 350°. Scoop out insides and mix with rest of ingredients. Fill potato shells and bake 20 minutes longer.

SWEET POTATO CASSEROLE FOR THANKSGIVING

6 red sweet potatoes   1 cup of raisins
1 cup of sugar   1 teaspoon of cinnamon
3 eggs   mini-marshmallows
1/4 cup of butter
1 cup of milk

Boil potatoes until tender. Drain. Mash until creamy. Add eggs, butter, milk, cinnamon, raisins, and nuts. Pour into baking dish and place marshmallows on top. Bake 30 minutes at 350°. Serve hot.

TOMATO CASSEROLE

Slice raw tomatoes in a pan. Slice green peppers and rings of onion over the tomatoes. Season with sugar, salt, and pepper. Smother with bread crumbs seasoned with salt, pepper and butter. Bake in moderate oven for 1 - 1 1/2 hours.

POTATOES AU GRATIN

4 boiled and diced potatoes   pepper
1/4 teaspoon of salt   paprika

Sauce:
1 cup of milk
1/2 cup of melted cheddar cheese
1 heaping tablespoon of flour blended with 2 tablespoons of butter

Cook the sauce ingredients together in a kettle until it forms a creamy sauce. Add diced potatoes, salt, pepper, and paprika. Heat until potatoes are tender.

GARDEN GREEN BEANS

3 tablespoons of butter   green beans from the garden (1 quart)
3 tablespoons of flour
2 cups of milk
1/4 pound of your favorite cheese

Cook your green beans until tender. Drain them and place in a casserole. In a saucepan, melt the butter, flour, milk, and cheese together. Pour over the green beans. Slice 3 hard boiled eggs over the mix, and crumble several slices of toasted bread over the mixture. Cover with cheese slices and cook at 350° until cheese slices melt.

GARDEN BEETS

1/3 cup of sugar   3 cups of fresh, cooked beets
1 tablespoon of cornstarch   2 tablespoons of butter
1 teaspoon of salt
1/4 cup of vinegar
1/4 cup of water

Blend sugar, cornstarch, and salt. Stir in vinegar and water. Mix until smooth. Bring blend to a boil and cook for five minutes. Add beets to hot mixture and allow to stand for 30 minutes. Just before serving, bring to a boil and add butter.

GREEN BEAN CASSEROLE

1 pound of hamburger   5 medium potatoes, boiled
1 small onion, chopped   1/2 cup of milk
1 pint of green beans, drained   1 egg
1 can of tomato sauce   1/2 cup of shredded cheese

Brown hamburger and onion. Drain off fat. Pour into a greased casserole dish. Add beans and stir in tomato sauce. Mash potatoes, milk, and egg together in a separate bowl. Mold potatoes in a ring shape over the bean-hamburger mix. Bake 30-40 minutes at 350°. Sprinkle a 1/2 cup of your favorite cheese over the potatoes.

CARROT BAKE

Cook 4 minutes in a pressure cooker:

1 quart of sliced carrots   1/4 cup of celery
1 teaspoon of salt

In a separate saucepan cook the following until nice and thick:

3 tablespoons of oleo   2 tablespoons of onions
3 tablespoons of flour   2 cups of milk, add to mix gradually
1/2 teaspoon of salt   dash of pepper
1 cup of cracker crumbs

Put cooked carrots into a buttered 2 quart casserole. Add thickened cream sauce. Sprinkle cracker crumbs on top. Bake for 45 minutes at 350°.

CORN BAKE

Corn dishes like these are commonly served to company during harvest season which begins in the late summer and runs through autumn.

2 eggs, separated   1/2 teaspoon of salt
3 cups of uncooked kernel corn   1/4 teaspoon of black pepper
3/4 cup of milk   1/2 cup of cracker crumbs
1/2 cup of sour cream   1/4 teaspoon of salt
2 tablespoons of melted butter
2 tablespoons of chopped pimento

Combine the beaten egg yolks with corn, spices, and milk. Blend well and pour into a buttered 2 quart casserole. Blend sour cream with stiffly beaten egg whites and fold into the corn mixture. Sprinkle the top with cracker crumbs mixed with melted butter and dot with pimento. Bake 1 hour at 350°.

AMISH DINNER SLAW

1 small head of cabbage
2 tart apples, chopped
1 medium onion
3 hard-boiled eggs
1/4 teaspoon of salt
1/4 cup of lemon juice

2 pimentos
2 tablespoons of sugar
1 teaspoon of dry mustard
1 tablespoon of melted butter
1/2 cup of whipped cream

Shred cabbage, and combine with apples, onion, and pimento. Grate egg yolks. Add salt, sugar, mustard, and butter. Add egg whites chopped fine. Stir in lemon juice, then add whipped cream and mix well.

ASPARAGUS LOAF

2 quarts of cooked asparagus
2 quarts of bread cubes
8 eggs
4 cups of milk
4 tablespoons of melted butter
2 teaspoons of salt

Combine all ingredients well in a mixing bowl. Pour into two loaf pans. Bake at 350° for about an hour.

SCALLOPED CORN

1 can of creamed corn
2 eggs
2 tablespoons of flour
1/3 cup of butter

1/2 cup of milk
1/2 cup of sugar
1/4 teaspoon of salt

Stir all together in a buttered casserole dish. Bake at 375° for 60 minutes.

CANDY

CHAPTER 8

FUDGE

1 can of evaporated milk   4 cups of sugar
4 sticks of margarine   1 -10 ounce bag of marshmallows
12 ounces of chocolate chips   1 teaspoon of vanilla

Boil milk, margarine, and sugar to soft ball stage. Then add
marshmallows, chips, and vanilla. Stir well, pour into a pan and let
harden.

PEANUTTY SQUARES

1 cup of peanut butter   Melt together peanut butter,
1 cup of peanuts   marshmallow creme, and
2 cups of marshmallow creme   margarine. When blended
4 cups of Cheerios™ cereal   together add Cheerios with
1 stick of margarine   one cup of brown sugar. Stir
1 cup of brown sugar   well and drop by teaspoon onto
                                  a cookie sheet. Chill.

PEANUT BUTTER BALLS

2 cups of crunchy peanut butter   1 pound of powdered sugar
3 cups of Rice Krispies™   1 stick of butter

Make size of walnuts and dip in chocolate. Let set for awhile, and they
are ready to serve.

PEANUT BUTTER CUPS

1 pound of margarine   3 pounds of powdered sugar
2 pounds of peanut butter

Mix margarine and peanut butter, then work in powdered sugar. Shape
into balls the size of big marbles and then dip in chocolate. Let set and
serve.

CHOCOLATE COATED PEANUTS

2 pounds of raw peanuts   a little paraffin, melted in chocolate
3 pounds of chocolate

Roast raw peanuts. Take out in air and dump back and forth until loose skins are out of bowl. Pour into melted chocolate. Stir. Drop by 1 and 2 peanuts onto a plate. Cool.

ROCKY ROAD SQUARES

3 pounds of milk chocolate   1/2 pound of soft butter
3 pounds of broken walnuts   10 ounces of mini-marshmallows

Melt chocolate and stir until creamy. Add butter and mix well. The mixture will be thick and warm. Add marshmallows and walnuts. Pour onto wax paper-lined cookie sheet. Press to about 3/4 of an inch thickness and cool. Cut into squares when it has cooled to room temperature.

CRUNCHY CEREAL CHOCOLATE BARS

1/3 cup of corn syrup
1-6 ounce package of butterscotch chips
4 cups of Kix™ cereal
1 1/2 cups of mini-marshmallows

Butter square 9X9X2 inch pan. Heat corn syrup to boiling point in a 3-quart saucepan. Remove from heat; stir in butterscotch chips until melted. Gradually fold in cereal until completely coated. Fold in marshmallows. Press mixture into a pan with buttered spoon. Let stand one hour. Cut into 2 1/4 inch bars. Makes 18 bars.

PEANUT BRITTLE

2 cups of sugar
1 cup of corn syrup
2 teaspoons of baking soda
1/2 cup of water

1/2 stick of butter
1 teaspoon of vanilla
1 pound of raw peanuts
pinch of salt

Mix the above ingredients - except for the soda. Cook until it gets hard in cold water. Add soda after the mixture gets hard. Spread on buttered pan. Break into pieces.

MINT PATTIES

1 box of powdered sugar
2 teaspoons of cream
1 tablespoon of butter
Melted semi-sweet chocolate

1 egg (unbeaten)
1 teaspoon of vanilla
3 drops of peppermint oil

Mix together all ingredients except for chocolate. Shape into patties and dip into melted chocolate. Let set and serve.

CARAMEL CORN

2 cups of brown sugar
2 sticks of oleo
popped pop corn

1/2 cup of light or dark corn syrup
1 teaspoon of baking soda

Mix and cook for 3-4 minutes on a high burner, stirring constantly. Remove from burner and add baking soda. Stir well, but quickly, until baking soda is blended in, about 2 more minutes. Pour over popped corn. Mix very well. This will coat 2 gallons of popped corn.

SODA CRACKER CANDY

2 cups of sugar
2/3 cup of milk

2 dozen soda crackers (crushed fine)
1-12 ounce package of butterscotch chips

Stir sugar into milk. Boil 3 to 5 minutes. Fold in crushed soda crackers and 1 package of butterscotch chips. Stir well. Pour into buttered pan and let set until cool.

MY MAPLE CANDY

8 ounces of cream cheese
8 ounces of oleo
melted milk chocolate

10 cups of powdered sugar
1 teaspoon of maple flavoring

Mix together. Chill until set. Make into patties. Dip into melted chocolate and chill again.

CHOCOLATE-COVERED CHERRIES

20 ounces of pitted cherries
1/4 pound of soft butter
1/2 cup of cherry juice

2 pounds of powdered sugar
Melted semi-sweet chocolate

Mix sugar, juice, and butter thoroughly (handles better if you let it cool for awhile, so after you mix it, chill it). Make small balls, press flat and cover cherries. Dip into chocolate within 2 hours or it will be hard to dip.

BUTTERSCOTCH SAUCE

1 cup of brown sugar
2 tablespoons of dark corn syrup

1/4 cup of whole milk
3 tablespoons of butter

Combine all ingredients, and over high heat stir until boiling. Lower heat and simmer for a few minutes. Pour over ice cream.

CHURCH WINDOWS FOR CHRISTMAS

12 ounces of semi-sweet chocolate
1 stick of oleo
1 package of colored marshmallows
1 cup of nut meats

Melt chocolate and oleo together until creamy. Fold in one package of colored marshmallows. Spread one cup of chopped nut meats on wax paper. Cover with marshmallow-chocolate mixture. Roll up like a jelly roll. Refrigerate until solid. Slice and serve.

RICE CANDY

2 cups of brown sugar
1/2 cup of maple-flavored corn syrup
1/4 cup of water
1 teaspoon of vinegar
2 teaspoons of butter
1 package of puffed rice

Cook all of the above ingredients, except the butter, for ten minutes, then put in 2 teaspoons of butter. Cool till a hard ball stage. Pour over 1 package of puffed rice.

CHOCOLATE PEANUT BUTTER BUDS

2 pounds of powdered sugar   1 stick of oleo
2 cups of peanut butter   2 1/2 cups of Rice Krispies
Melted semi-sweet chocolate

Mix together everything except for the chocolate. Form into balls and dip into the chocolate. Let set. Can be stored in a sealed plastic container or chilled.

HOLIDAY WREATHS

1/2 cup of margarine
6 cups of mini-marshmallows
1/2 teaspoon of vanilla

1 teaspoon of green food coloring
6 cups of corn flakes cereal

Melt margarine in a 3-quart saucepan. Add marshmallows and cook over low heat, stirring constantly, until marshmallows are melted and mixture is syrupy. Remove from heat. Stir in vanilla and green food coloring. Add corn flakes; stir until well-coated. Shape into rings.

CORN FLAKE CANDY

1 cup of sugar
1/2 cup of cream
1 cup of nut meats

1 cup of light corn syrup
4 cups of corn flakes

Cook sugar, syrup, and cream to a soft ball stage. Then stir in the cereal and nuts. Mix well, and drop by spoon onto waxed paper. Makes 4 dozen.

CANDY EGGS FOR EASTER

3 cups of white sugar
1 cup of milk and cream
1/2 cup of light corn syrup
2 tablespoons of butter

a pinch of salt
melted semi-sweet chocolate

Bring sugar, milk, corn syrup, and butter to a soft ball point. Cool. Then stir until thick. Shape into mini-eggs and cool. Dip in melted chocolate and chill.

CANNING AND
MISCELLANEOUS

CHAPTER 9

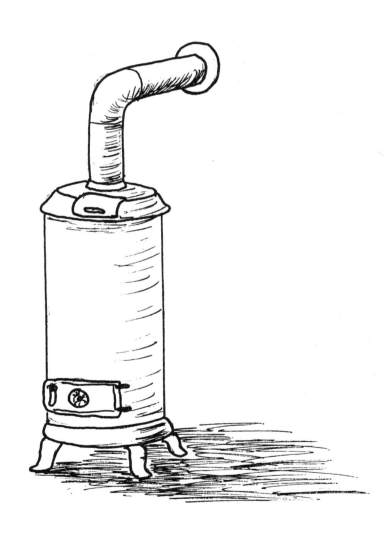

CANNING

It is autumn, and the cellar has been completed for another year. Fruits, vegetables, jams, jellies, and preserves are all canned. Meat is usually done in the wintertime, although chicken is done during the fall. Chicken can be cut-up into pieces and again it can be cooked and taken from the bone and then processed. The jar can then be opened to make dressings, soups, and stews.

Butchering of beef and pork is usually done in the wintertime. Beef can be cut-up into chunks, or ground for hamburger and steaks. Beef bones can be cooked and then the meat removed from them and processed for soups or stews.

Pork has a variety of foods to be processed into, like sausage, pork chops, ham, and bacon (side meat). We usually sugar-cure our hams and bacon. The meat and some of the vegetables such as corn and green beans are put under pressure. Tomatoes and fruits are processed in an open cooker. Tomatoes made into juice is considered good to drink around here. As the saying goes: "tomato juice is a poor man's orange juice."

Processed cherries, blueberries, pumpkin, apples, and other fruits are used in pies and cakes, or to make cobblers. Fruits such as peaches, pineapples, strawberries, plums, or pears can be served plain in their juices.

Home-canned foods will keep for many years if done in the correct and clean way. Not having the jars washed clean will cause them to open and spoil later on. The jars have to be washed clean in hot, soapy water and rinsed well in hot water. Fill jars of whatever you are processing, one inch from the top. Clean the top of the jar with a clean, damp dishcloth. Wipe off the top lip of the jars before putting on the lid, and screw-band.

CANNING TERMS AND INFORMATION

RAW OR COLD PACK: Pack cold, raw vegetables (except corn, lima beans, and peas) tightly into containers and cover with boiling water.

HOT PACK: Preheat vegetables in boiling water or cooking liquid and then pack into jars.

IMPORTANT: Canning is very a vital part of Amish culture. This chapter is presented so readers can sample this area of Amish culture. People unfamiliar with canning procedures should not attempt these recipes. Canning classes are offered at community colleges, and your local county extension agent can answer any canning questions.

Those pressure cookers are so handy for food processing. The meats were usually in open cookers for three hours and now with the pressure cooker, it only takes half that time.

Well, good luck with your home-canning.

CANNING POTATOES

We use the little potatoes. Take the skins off. Put in quart or 2-quart jars, adding 1/2 teaspoon to a quart. Then add hot water to fill jars. Cold pack for 2 hours or pressure cook 1/2 hour (not more).

PORK AND BEANS TO CAN

8 pounds navy beans
1 large onion
1/3 cup salt
4 quarts tomato juice
1/2 teaspoon pepper
1 teaspoon of cinnamon

1 1/2 pounds cut-up bacon or wieners
3 cups of white sugar
4 cups of brown sugar
1 teaspoon of dry mustard
1-26 ounce bottle of catsup
4 tablespoons of cornstarch

Soak beans overnight. Cook them until soft. Mix the rest of the ingredients together and cook a few minutes. Then add to beans and mix well. Put into jars and seal. Cold pack 1 1/2 hours. Makes approximately 17 quarts.

VEGETABLE SOUP TO CAN

1 quart of potatoes
1 quart of carrots
1 quart of celery
1 quart of corn
1 quart of peas
1 quart of onions

1 quart of soup beans
6-7 quarts of tomato juice
1 cup of elbow spaghetti
1/2 cup of sugar
1 1/2 pounds of hamburger
1 tablespoon of chili powder

Cold pack 90 minutes in a pressure cooker (10 pounds of pressure). Pour into jars and seal tightly. Makes around 15 quarts of soup.

TOMATO SOUP TO CAN

1/2 bushel of tomatoes
1 stalk of parsley
2 cups of sugar
12 onions

2 or 3 green peppers
1/2 cup of salt
2 stalks of celery
2 cups of flour

Cook tomatoes, onions, green peppers, parsley, and celery. Put through a strainer, then add flour, sugar, and salt. Heat to almost boiling. Put in jars and cold pack 1 hour. When heating to serve, add milk and butter.

GRAPE MOLASSES

1 pint of light corn syrup   1 pint of grape juice
3 pounds of sugar

Boil about three minutes. Pour into jars and seal. Raspberry juice may be used in place of the grape juice.

PENNSYLVANIA CANNED TOMATO SOUP

1/2 bushel of tomatoes   11 sprigs of parsley
2 quarts of water   14 stalks of celery
7 medium onions   14 tablespoons of melted butter
16 tablespoons of sugar   14 tablespoons of flour
4 tablespoons of paprika   8 teaspoons of salt
1 pint of water

Bring sliced, peeled tomatoes and two quarts of water to a boil. Add chopped onions, diced celery, and parsley. Cook until vegetables are well done. Put through a sieve. Put back in pan to cook. Add butter, flour, sugar, salt, and paprika. Stir. Then add one pint of water, cook until thick. Strain and put into sterilized jars. Seal. Dilute with milk or water when you open jars to heat.

TOMATO CATSUP

1 gallon of ripe tomatoes   2 teaspoons of salt
1 large onion   1 cup of sugar
1 tablespoon of pickling spice   1 cup of vinegar

Chop tomatoes, cook with onion and pickling spice until well done. Drain off the juice. Put through sieve, add salt, sugar, and vinegar to tomatoes. Cook until the tomato mixture is thick. This mixture is your catsup. The juice can be used in chili or vegetable soup.

BEET JELLY

5 pounds of ripe beets
2 tablespoons of lemon juice
2-3 ounce boxes of raspberry gelatin

7 cups of sugar
2 boxes of powdered pectin

Wash 5 pounds of ripe beets. Cut off the tops and ends. Put in pan and cover with water. Bring to a boil and cook for 1 hour. Pour juice off and strain. Add lemon juice and pectin to 6 cups of beet juice. Bring mixture to a boil and add 7 cups of sugar and the dry raspberry gelatin. Boil 10 minutes. Remove from heat, skim jelly and pour into hot sterile jelly jars. Cover with a thin layer of paraffin. Let cool.

TOMATO JELLY

5 cups of tomato juice
5 cups of sugar

Lard the size of an egg
6 ounces of cherry Jello™

Boil lard for 15 minutes, remove from heat and stir into 6 ounces of cherry Jello. Pour into a jar and seal at once.

TOMATO COCKTAIL

1/2 bushel of tomatoes
6 large mangos
6 large onions
parsley

1 bunch of celery
6 red beets
carrots

Cook these together and put through strainer. Add:

2 cups of sugar
1/2 cup of salt (scant)

3 lemons
cloves

Bring to rolling boil. Put into jars and cold pack for 20 minutes. Makes 10-12 quarts.

PEAR BUTTER

Rinse pears, but don't peel. Slice and add a small amount of water to begin cooking. Cook until very soft. Press through sieve. To each cup of pulp, add 1/2 cup of sugar. A nice spice, such as cinnamon, 1/2 teaspoon for every 3 cups of pear pulp can be added. Cook in kettle until thick, stirring often to prevent scorching. Spoon into a sterilized jar to 1/2 inch from the top. Screw cap on very, very tightly. Boil jar in water for 10 minutes, then store.

CHOW CHOW

This dish has Oriental origins, and is a good example of how the Amish have "borrowed" cooking ideas from other cultures and incorporated them into their own. The Amish are now well-known for their version of chow chow.

1 quart of green string beans
1 quart of chopped celery
1 quart of kidney beans
1 quart of yellow corn
1 quart of diced carrots
10 diced red peppers
1 quart of water

1 quart of navy beans
4 small onions, diced
3 pounds of sugar
2 quarts of white vinegar
2 teaspoons of mustard seed
2 teaspoons of celery seed
2 tablespoons of pickling spices

Cook all the vegetables until nice and tender. Drain through a colander. Mix sugar, mustard seed, celery seed, vinegar, and water until it forms a syrupy mixture. Put the pickling spice in a cloth bag and immerse in the syrup. Boil the syrup. Remove the pickle spice bag and stir in cooked vegetables. Boil them again. Pack chow chow into jars and seal tightly. Add salt for seasoning.

SWEET DILL PICKLES

1 quart of vinegar
1 pint of water
4 cups of white sugar

1/4 cup of salt
4 onions
pickles

Cook this together for a few minutes on high. Then fill 5 one-quart jars with sliced pickles. Put 3 garlic seeds in a jar then pour hot vinegar mixture over pickles. Cold pack for five minutes.

DILL PICKLES

1/2 cup of vinegar
1 1/2 cups of water
1 tablespoon of salt

2 teaspoons of dill seed
1 quart of pickles

Boil vinegar, water, and salt. Put pickles and dill seed in a one-quart jar and pour hot vinegar mixture over pickles and seal.

CHILLED PICKLES

7 cups of unpeeled, sliced cucumbers
1 cup of diced green peppers
1 cup of sliced onions

Mix these in a bowl. Do not mash.

Brine:

1 cup of vinegar
2 teaspoons of salt

2 cups of sugar
1 tablespoon of celery seed

Do not heat. Dissolve sugar in vinegar and add celery seed and salt. Stir. Pour over sliced cucumbers. Cover and refrigerate. Let chill for 24 hours before eating.

CORN RELISH

5 cups of cut corn	2 cups of cut celery
4 large onions	3 cups of shredded cabbage
2 peppers, cut fine	3 cups of sugar
2 tablespoons of salt	1 pint of vinegar
3/4 teaspoon of turmeric powder	2 tablespoons of ground mustard

Put all in a large kettle and heat well. Stir occasionally. Can and seal.

ALL WEEK SWEET PICKLES

7 pounds of medium-sized cucumbers	8 cups of sugar
water to cover	2 tablespoons of salt
2 tablespoons of mixed pickle spice	1 quart of vinegar

Wash cucumbers and cover them with boiling water. Let set 24 hours and drain. Repeat each day for 4 days, using fresh water each time (boiling water). On fifth day, cut cucumbers in 1/4 inch slices. Combine vinegar, sugar, salt, and spices: bring liquid to a boil and pour over cucumbers. Let set 24 hours. Drain syrup and bring to a boil. Pour over cucumbers. Repeat on the sixth day and the last day, drain off the syrup again, then bring to a boil. Add cucumber slices and bring to the boiling point. Pack into hot jars and seal.

CANNED CUCUMBER SALAD

25 to 30 medium-sized cucumbers	5 cups of sugar
8 large white onions	2 tablespoons of mustard seed
2 large sweet peppers	1 teaspoon of turmeric powder
1/2 cup of salt	1/2 teaspoon of cloves
5 cups of cider vinegar	

Wash cucumbers and slice as thin as possible. Chop onions and peppers and combine cucumbers and salt. Let stand three hours, then drain. Combine vinegar, sugar, and spices in a kettle and bring to a boil. Add drained cucumber mixture. Heat thoroughly, but don't boil. Pack tightly into jars and seal at once.

SAUERKRAUT

Shred cabbage and put into jars. Add 1 teaspoon of salt and 1 tablespoon of vinegar for every one quart of cabbage. Fill jars with cold water. Put lids on and turn tight. Put in a cellar for 2 months, then it is ready to eat.

RHUBARB JAM

5 cups of rhubarb, cut fine
4 cups of sugar
6 ounce package of whatever flavor of gelatin you prefer

Mix rhubarb and sugar and let set overnight. In the morning, boil for 5 minutes. Then add gelatin. Put in jars and seal.

ONION DIP

1/2 cup of mayonnaise   3 tablespoons of onion, grated
1/2 cup of sour cream   Pinch of salt to taste
2 tablespoons of milk

Mix all of the above ingredients well. Chill.

BRAUNSCHWEIGER CHEESE BALL

1/2 pound of braunschweiger   1/4 teaspoon onion salt
1 large package of cream cheese
1 tablespoon of Worcestershire sauce

Mix ingredients until smooth and creamy. Refrigerate. Serve with sliced olives on top, if desired.

VERENA'S CHEESE BALL

Dried beef (two packages)
Cream cheese (3 eight ounce packages)
One small onion
Salt

Chop-up the dried beef and mix with the cream cheese. Add onions to taste and sprinkle with salt. Serve with crackers.

SANDWICH SPREAD

12 green tomatoes
12 green mangoes
12 mangoes
2 large onions

1 cup of prepared mustard
1/2 cup of sugar
1/4 cup salt
1 tablespoon of celery seed

Stir this all together and boil for 15 minutes. Take off stove and add 1 quart of your favorite salad dressing. Mix and put back on real low heat so it won't boil. Can and seal while hot.

TARTAR SAUCE

12 large green tomatoes
12 small green peppers
4 medium onions
1 cup of prepared mustard
1 cup of vinegar

3 cups of sugar
4 teaspoons of salt
1/2 cup of flour
1 quart of salad dressing (any kind)

Chop tomatoes, peppers, and onions until fine. Drain. Pour enough boiling water over the top of the mixture to cover; then let stand at least 2 minutes. Heat water mixture, then add mustard, vinegar, sugar, and salt. Stir well and boil for 15 minutes. Make a paste of water and flour and add to the above mixture. Cook 10 minutes. While hot, add salad dressing. Stir well and place in glass jars. Seal while hot. Makes 10 pints.

ROOT BEER

1 gallon of warm water
1 3/4 cups of sugar

4 tablespoons of root beer extract
1 tablespoon of yeast

Mix all ingredients together and pour into a gallon jug. Cover and set in the sun for 3 hours or more. Refrigerate overnight.

LIME PUNCH

4 packages of lemon-lime Kool-Aid™
3 cups of sugar
1 1/2 quarts of Sprite™
2 quarts of orange juice

3 quarts of water
1 quart of pineapple juice

Mix all together, except for the Sprite. Add the Sprite just before serving. Makes 2 gallons.

BREAKFAST NOG

1 egg
1 cup of milk
1 tablespoon of honey or sugar
1 teaspoon of vanilla
A pinch of nutmeg or cinnamon

Blend together and chill.

EGG NOG

2 eggs
2 cups of milk (chilled)

4 tablespoons of vinegar
1/2 teaspoon of vanilla

Mix well and serve cold.

Hint: Although the Amish do not have electric blenders, this recipe would work well if blended in an electric blender.

SUMMER DAY PUNCH

1 gallon of any flavored fruit drink   1 quart of ginger ale
1/2 gallon of orange sherbet

Beat frozen sherbet into the fruit drink. Add ginger ale and serve.

RED PUNCH

12 ounces of frozen lemonade
12 ounces of frozen orange juice
32 ounce can of Hawaiian Punch™
1 quart of 7-up™
1 1/2 quarts of water

Mix the ingredients together very well and chill. Serves 25.

FRUIT PUNCH

1 can of Hawaiian Punch
1 (12 ounce) can of frozen orange juice
2 packages of strawberry Kool-Aid™
1 quart of water
1 can of pineapple juice
3 orange juice cans of water
1 cup of white sugar

Stir well until blended, chill and serve.

GRAPE JUICE

For every 2 quarts of grapes add 1/2 cup of chilled water. Boil until soft. Remove from fire. Strain through a cheesecloth. To each quart jar, add 1 cup of sugar. Cold pack for 10 minutes. When you open a jar, add equal amount of water as juice. Chill and serve.

THE BUDGET

Established on May 15, 1890, *The Budget* serves as one of the few links between Amish and Mennonite communities across the country. From Rexford, Montana to Kitchener, Ontario to Newport, Maine and Sarasota, Florida, *The Budget* serves as a community crier, passing information about births, deaths, weddings, and life experiences. *The Budget* is a weekly paper, and most Amish feel a twinge of anticipation as they head for the mailbox on "Budget day."

The paper is based in Sugarcreek, Ohio in the heart of Amish country. The Amish writers who fill *The Budget* with their weekly writings are called scribes. Elizabeth has been a scribe for over 40 years, reporting weekly on events in the Coblentz household and community. To the non-Amish, the letters may seem like just a boring tangle of names, but to an Amish person reading *The Budget* in a faraway place, it is an invaluable source of information. *The Budget* is full of such letters each week, and helps to make Amish individuals feel connected to the community at large.

The lesser-known, Old-Order Amish-owned, *Die Botschaft* is a newspaper similar in format to *The Budget*. It is published in Lancaster County, Pennsylvania and was started to provide an information outlet to Old Order Amish people only. Some Amish people became upset about the increasing number of Mennonites and non-Amish Pennsylvania Dutch scribes contributing to the English-owned *Budget*. *Die Botschaft* features letters solely from Old Order Amish people.

The following is a Budget entry from the week of Elizabeth's wedding. To most people it would seem like a boring, and confusing, tangle of names. But to people in the Amish community, separated by miles and a lack of quick communication, it serves as a fun and informative source of "who is doing what?" Often word of a wedding doesn't reach a relative until someone writes about it in The Budget.

OCTOBER 21, 1957 -- Nice and cool weather. Lots of flu and colds are around. Different schools are closed on account of the flu.

Thursday, October 17, was the wedding day of Ben A. Coblentz and Elizabeth Graber (the writer). They were married by Bishop Mose M. Miller from Indiana. Wedding church was held at Chris Schwartz's and wedding supper was served at the bride's home, Amos Graber's. Their attendants: Toby Swartzentruber and Lovina Graber; and Dan Hilty and Barbara Schwartz. Tablewaiters were: Elmer Schwartz and Emma Graber; David Graber and Salome Graber; Levi Schwartz and Barbara Wickey; David Schwartz and Ada K. Hilty; Joe Schwartz and Leah Wickey; La Verne Schwartz and Maggie Schwartz and Chris Neuenschwander and Anna Schwartz.

Uncle, Mr. and Mrs. Mose Coblentz and two daughters from Hartville, Ohio spent Thursday and Friday evening around here. They attended the above wedding and were Friday dinner guests at the writer's home. Also, others here for dinner were: Aunt Mrs. Milo Yoder, Ernest Eichers, Mr. and Mrs. John Hilty and Daughter Mary and Mr. and Mrs. Albert Coblentz Sr.; Mrs. Joe Schwartz and sons, Mrs. Dan S. Wickey and daughter Barbara, Sam C. Schwartz and sons, and Toby Swartzentruber.

Each church was held at Amos Grabers on November 3.

South church is to be held at the Deacon Dan J. Schwartz's next Sunday. South church was was held at John H. Eichers where a preacher was ordained.

Recently, a son was born to Mr. and Mrs. Emanuel Schwartz of Ohio. He was named Emanuel Clyde. Mrs. Schwartz was formerly Kathy Coblentz.

Mr. and Mrs. Andy Coblentz of Indiana attended the above wedding of his brother Ben.

Grandpa Chris Neuenschwander's family were afternoon callers today at Amos Grabers.

AMISH COMMUNITIES

There are Amish communities throughout the country -- 22 states and Ontario. There are no Amish settlements in Europe. Some of the larger Amish settlements include:

Holmes County, Ohio
La Grange County, Indiana
Lancaster County, Pennsylvania
Montezuma, Georgia
Pinecraft-Sarasota, Florida

Kitchener, Ontario
Arthur, Illinois

The Amish welcome new visitors into their communities. Conversation is one of the chief means of entertainment for the Amish, so exchanging words and ideas with new people can be an enjoyable experience for the Amish, as well as for a visitor. However, the Amish are not tourist attractions. They are trying to live their lives just like anyone else.

"How would you like it if someone came up to you and snapped your picture without asking?" said a Hillsdale County, Michigan Amish man. Whatever behavior would be considered rude to your neighbor also applies when visiting the Amish. The Amish religion strictly forbids photographs of church members. The Golden Rule applies when visiting Amish country.

Some common courtesies to observe when traveling through Amish settlements, include:

1) Never take photos of Amish people.

2) When approaching an Amish home, try to talk to the man first. Women tend to shy away from initial contact.

3) Be courteous and cautious when sharing roads with buggies.

PRAYER TO LIVE BY

Blessed are the poor in spirit,
for theirs is the kingdom of heaven
Blessed are they that mourn:
for they shall be comforted.
Blessed are the meek:
for they shall inherit the earth.
Blessed are they which do hunger and thirst
after righteousness:
for they shall be filled.
Blessed are the merciful:
for they shall obtain mercy.
Blessed are the pure in heart:
for they shall see God.
Blessed are the peacemakers:
for they shall be called the children of God.
These are the lessons that Jesus taught in the
"Sermon on the Mount."

December, 1945, my teacher, Pauline Kizer, gave as a Christmas gift to all her students, a book of "The Lord's Prayer." She taught the first four grades at a country school which was called No. 5. So this book has been treasured since the time I received it.

INDEX

PIES

Apple, 84
Banana, 90
Bob Andy, 82
Bread, 83
Chocolate mocha, 91
Choo fly, 83
Coconut, 91
Coconut cream, 92
Corn meal, 85
Cream, 83
Custard, 88
Grape, 90
Green tomato, 89
Lemon fluff, 86
Lemon, 86
Millionaire, 80
Nut, 92
Oatmeal, 84
Peach cream, 87
Peanut butter, 89
Pecan, Indiana, 85
Pecan, Levi's, 85
Pineapple sponge, 90
Raisin, 92
Rhubarb, 84
Rhurbarb, 84
Strawberry, 91

COOKIES

Angel, 79
Broomstick, 76
Christmas, 74
Chocolate chip, 75
Cry Baby, 78
Haystack, 78
Molasses, 73
Monster, 72
No-bake, 73
Oatmeal chewy, 74
Oatmeal, icebox, 74
Peanut butter, 76
Pinwheel, 78

COOKIES (CONTINUED)

Quaker, 72
Ranger, 77
Sugar, 76
Squash, 74
Told-you-so, 77
Whoopie pies, 75
Yoder's, 79

CAKES

Angel food, 98
Buttermilk, 100
Butterscotch, 100
Cheesecake, 96
Chocolate angel food, 99
Chocolate chip cake, 99
Coffeecake, Ben's, 51
Coffecake, Nancy's, 58
Eicher cake, 96
Peach upside-down, 98
Pineapple upside-down, 99
Red devil's, 97
Rhubarb, 95
Salad dressing, 95
Vaniilla, 100
Frosting for cake, 96

DESSERT SNACKS

Puddings:
  Bread, 67
  Cinnamon, 64
  Date nut, 68
  Plum, 67
  Tapioca, 66
Other desserts:
Cherry cobbler, 64
Cherry crunch, 69
Chocolate chip brownies, 66
Chocolate mousse, 70
Dollies, 70
Heavenly bits, 70
Pumpkin bars, 68
Rhubarb butter crunch, 69